ARCHITECTURE
OF
THE VICTORIAN
ERA
OF KINGSTON UPON HULL

ARCHITECTURE
OF
THE VICTORIAN
ERA
OF KINGSTON UPON HULL

Being a study of the principal buildings erected in Hull
1830-1914

Ian N. Goldthorpe

Edited by
Margaret Sumner

Highgate of Beverley

Highgate Publications (Beverley) Limited
2005

British Library Cataloguing in Publication Data.
A catalogue record for this book is available from the British Library.

© 2005 Ian N. Goldthorpe

Ian N. Goldthorpe asserts the moral right to be identified as the author of this work.

ISBN 1 902645 42 1

Published by

Highgate of Beverley

Highgate Publications (Beverley) Limited
4 Newbegin, Beverley, HU17 8EG. Telephone (01482) 886017

Printed by Highgate Print Limited
4 Newbegin, Beverley, HU17 8EG. Telephone (01482) 886017

FOREWORD

by IVAN HALL

In retrospect few will doubt that the city of Hull reached its peak of wealth and influence during the 19th century, building of course on the firm foundations of its long past. The improvements of the Victorian and Edwardian periods however determined the shape of the city as we know it today.

The name of Kingston upon Hull recalls the astute decision of Edward I, who foresaw the practical advantages that could follow a planned development at the junction of the rivers Hull and Humber. The site was well placed for both commercial life and purposes of defence, and the sequence of town walls that followed were planned and built on so generous a scale that there was no urgency to build beyond them until the last quarter of the 18th century. By that time Hull had secured its place as an interchange between foreign ports, especially those of northern Europe, and the rapidly improving network of inland waterways. These penetrated deep into the Midland counties via the Trent and its tributaries, into the heart of the Yorkshire Ridings via the Aire and the Ouse and their associated waterways, and perhaps most importantly via the late Georgian canal system that linked Manchester and Liverpool in the west to Hull on the east side of England. By such means, the two great areas of high industrial expansion, the Black Country and central Lancashire, fed and were fed by trading connections significant to Hull.

Overseas, Hull's merchanting families had carefully fostered, by long-standing personal contacts, their counterparts in the principal ports from Russia to Spain and Portugal. Through residence abroad, successive generations of young Hull merchants learnt the languages, the customs and the market opportunities offered by the different parts of Europe. They were thus in a position to encourage the development and supply of a wide variety of goods and services. The practical education abroad of the sons of Hull's leading families inevitably meant that local manufactures were tinged with an unmistakable Continental influence, whether such products were to be exported or consumed at home in Hull and its hinterland. For example, the brick and stone counterparts of Holy Trinity, Hull, can be found in the towns and cities of the Low Countries and North Germany. Similarly, the cut and moulded Renaissance brickwork of houses such as Wilberforce House or that formerly in Dagger Lane is comparable in style to examples found among the 17th-century architecture of Holland. By the 18th and 19th centuries, however, it was the influence of France that proved to be the strongest, as witnessed by the splendid staircase for Maister House in the High Street, or the great volumes of Parisian-style furniture made by the eminent firm of Richardson during the last half of the Victorian era, which can still be seen at nearby Burton Constable, where it is often taken as 'made in France'.

Hull's furniture-making industry flourished for a century and a half, and the best pieces were the equal of anything made by London rivals. The trade was slowing down before the First World War, and it did not recover effectively after the closure of the principal export markets during the war.

Cotton manufacture was another, now largely forgotten, Hull industry. Given the town's trade with the Baltic and North Sea ports, it seemed to make sense to manufacture cotton goods during the 1830s and 1840s, especially since Hull families such as the Peases and their relations the Heywoods, had well-established connections with the Liverpool raw cotton trade. First the canals, and then the railways, made it easier to transport the raw material to Hull, where labour was comparatively cheap. In 1845 the newly built mills of the Kingston Cotton Company equalled in size those found in the Pennine valleys; however, after a brave start, the industry faltered and new trades helped to take its place. For example, there was the expansion of the fishing industry from the 1850s until recent times, and the growth of the much older shipbuilding and ship-fitting industries. In the latter the main changes were from sail to steam and from wood to iron ships, the experience of the furniture-makers being put to good use in the creation of the luxurious interiors for many of the passenger ships that plied between Hull and the Continent. Shipbuilding, ship-fitting and furniture-making also encouraged yet another Hull trade, the importation of European and, from the 1760s, exotic timbers. One side effect of the easy availability of exotic timber was the encouragement of the wood carver's skills, especially when the substitution of iron for wood released the ship carver for work on the thousands of new houses built in the expanding High Victorian suburbs.

Thereafter, the number of carvers declined, their industry being replaced by that of cement making. For example, the earlier generations of the Earle family had been stonemasons and sculptors (one of whom, Thomas, had achieved national recognition), but the living from the fine arts could be precarious, especially in the provinces, and one branch of the Earle family foresaw a steady demand for cement products. An outlet was that of pre-cast ornaments that could be used in place of carved wood for the fronts of houses of every size in the Hull area, where good building stone was scarce. A mass produced, synthetic material such as cast cement often replaced hand worked, natural materials.

This desire for cheap but abundant ornament found another expression throughout late Victorian and Edwardian Hull, where decorative tilework was used in every context. The researches of Josie

Montgomery have shown that in this era of free trade, Hull's architects and builders as eagerly used tiles from the factories of Holland, France or Spain, as those from English potteries. Hygienic advantages were also found in the glazed fireclays and terracottas produced in Leeds, by firms such as Burmantofts, and these products too enliven and enrich the façades of both commercial and public buildings. One need only mention here the terracotta and tilework fronts of so many Hull public houses and, more startlingly, of churches such as Newland Congregational church, whose terracotta tower decorations included eight overlife-size statues of Nonconformist worthies in contemporary dress.

The shortage of stone also prompted the widespread early Victorian use of stucco, painted in simulation of the real thing, and of the pale grey-yellow bricks made from the seam of gault clay that cuts across the Humber basin or obtained in later years from as far away as Wales. Unlike stucco, gault clay brickwork presents a long-lasting surface though the tougher, later brickwork is, typically, of a harsher yellow colour. Some architects such as in the case of George Street, made play with multicoloured brickwork laid in formal patterns as in the interior decoration of All Saints', Margaret Street, which was perhaps Hull's finest Victorian church. A similar, but less impressive, patterning in brick can still be seen at St Matthew's, Anlaby Road.

Perhaps inevitably, the majority of Church of England churches built in Hull during the 19th century belonged to the Gothic Revival and formed an intentional contrast to the even greater number of Nonconformist churches and chapels. Of the latter none had a more splendid composition than the Wesleyan chapel in Great Thornton Street, whose wide Corinthian portico with eight columns intentionally recalls those of the National Gallery or University College in London. H. F. Lockwood's other major contributions to the architecture of Hull included the now demolished Congregational chapel in Albion Street, with its massive Greek Doric portico, and the charming and finely detailed chapel built within what was once the garden of Hull Trinity House. Lockwood almost certainly designed the finest of Hull's early Victorian town houses, that for James Alderson, next to Albion Street chapel. The house has now been refurbished as The Institute. With its screens of Ionic and Corinthian columns and its array of sculpture after the Danish artist Bertel Thorwaldsen, this interior had the self-conscious handsomeness of a public building; after long neglect little more than the original shell remained. Lockwood's remodelling of the Royal Infirmary has wholly gone and the work of his pupil Cuthbert Brodrick has suffered similarly. Brodrick's Hull Town Hall of 1862 has given place to the present Guildhall, and his Royal Institution was first blitzed and afterwards demolished.

Brodrick was passed over in favour of Christopher Wray in the competition for the Hull Dock Offices of 1869, and no Victorian building in the city boasts so opulent a concentration of surface decoration. Here, while the *scagliola* columns of the Court Room might also be found elsewhere, the brilliant figuring of the pine doors are clear reminders of Hull's pre-eminent place in the Baltic timber trade. This, the third Dock Office, provided the nucleus of the major improvement in the late Victorian period. The outcome was to be Queen Victoria Square with the City Hall (designed by the City Architect, Joseph Hirst, 1903-9) opposite and the Ferens Art Gallery (designed by Cooke & Davies) nearby to the south. This same spirit determined the Edwardian rebuilding of the Guildhall in a strongly French style. Regrettably the City fathers here turned their back on the long waterside frontage of Queen's Dock and instead sited the building along a new artery which then, and even more so now, makes it difficult to appreciate the real grandeur of Sir Edwin Cooper's principal façade.

Sadly, one may think of the Custom House or the Four Courts overlooking the Liffey in Dublin to realise the nature of the lost opportunity. The interior is notable for the marble-floored corridors, an echo of Venetian painting, and the marvellous array of bold oak carving scattered through the principal rooms. In recent years, due to the clearance of buildings, a new and impressive view of the Guildhall and Post Office was temporarily opened up on the east side. Edwardian bravura was extended to the ranges of shops and commercial premises built to line the new streets, giving vistas punctuated by domed and turreted cornerpieces, features that a decade or so earlier, had been largely confined to a group of Board Schools designed by William Botterill and later by Botterill and his young partner, John Bilson. These turrets or belfries in miniature recall the second phase of the Dutch influence on the city's architecture. Sadly these belfries too are disappearing. Mr Goldthorpe's book shows ten belfries on one page, opposing it with views of the Dutch houses that are the most remarkable feature of the Avenues district.

Mr Goldthorpe's thesis was undertaken in 1955, that is at a time when few students cared much for Victorian architecture and even less for the daunting task of recording its highlights. Simply to look through the illustrations is to realise that what began as a study is now in effect a memorial volume for so much has been demolished or mutilated in the interim. The chapels are now a tithe of their former number, and they went first. Then churches followed and to a lesser degree the schools, losses that reflected the process of comprehensive redevelopment, and the decanting of population from the inner city to the outer suburbs. What has gone are the accents of the cityscape, the varied shapes, textures and materials, the undoubted wealth of craftsmanship, the unexpected or even bizarre incident; items that there is now no way of matching, for neither money nor skills are forthcoming.

This publication brings to light a pioneering study of a largely vanished heritage, but one fully meriting sympathetic consideration. Though new facts have since emerged and new sources of material have become available to the historian, the overall picture that is here presented, of Hull as it was in 1955, cannot be diminished.

PREFACE

It was on 6 September 1948 that I started my architectural career by being articled to Harold Conyers Robinson, the Senior Partner of Gelder and Kitchen, who was a nephew of the late Sir Alfred Gelder, the founder of the firm. Con, as he was usually known, had been acquainted with me ever since I was born since he and his parents were our next door neighbours in Anlaby Park.

During my five years of articles I was a part-time student at the Hull School of Architecture and was especially grateful to the late Douglas Potter, the Junior Partner, for his insistence upon accurate and neat draughtsmanship and clear lettering. Similarly Alan Bray, later to become the Senior Partner of the firm, was a great help and inspiration to me, also encouraging me to join the Hull Art Club, as a result of which on one occasion I had some watercolours hung in the Ferens Art Gallery. Working with Gelder and Kitchen was a great experience for me since at that time the firm were involved in many large industrial projects such as the Baltic Flour Mills at Gateshead for Messrs Joseph Rank [now Baltic Art Gallery].

On completion of my articles I went fulltime to the Hull School of Architecture in order to complete my course. Architecture of the Victorian Era of Kingston upon Hull was my thesis written as part of my Royal Institute of British Architects final examination. My examiner was Professor Sir Albert Richardson, then architect to St Paul's Cathedral; he was responsible for repairs to the cathedral after wartime bombing, and he also designed the new high altar and the *baldachino* over it. Later he designed the astronomical clock in the north transept of York Minster. It was a real delight meeting him at the Royal Institute of British Architects Headquarters in London, and I was especially touched later to learn that I had been awarded a distinction for my thesis which, I believe, was quite a rare honour in those days.

In his series *The Buildings of England*, Sir Nikolaus Pevsner used this thesis when writing the Hull section of the volume covering *Yorkshire: York and the East Riding*, revised in 1995, by David Neave. Since then there have been two serious attempts to publish it. The first was by the former Hull College of Technology in Queen's Gardens. Mrs Basu from the printing department contacted me and we had several meetings regarding publication. Sadly, she was tragically killed in a road accident and no further progress was made. The second was by Humberside County Council when, shortly after 1974, Chris Knowles, the County Heritage Officer, contacted me regarding the possibility of publication. He updated the text and also arranged for Ivan Hall who, with his late wife Elisabeth, was the author of the excellent architectural guides, *Historic Beverley* and *Georgian Hull*, to write the foreword. Sadly we did not get as far as publication before Humberside was abolished in 1996. At this time Hull became a unitary authority, assumed responsibility for libraries and set up the Kingston Press.

However, Hull City Council have been unable to fit the publication of my thesis into their programme, and so I have decided to ask Highgate Publications of Beverley to publish the thesis in book form at my own expense since my success in life has largely been due to my formative years in the great city of Kingston upon Hull, and this is the least, I feel, that I can do in return.

Written half a century ago, many of the buildings described, some in considerable detail, have now been lost for ever. Although most of Hull's greatest and finest buildings which were in good order in the 1950s, at the time of my research, are still intact and very well maintained, many of the lesser buildings have been much altered and changed beyond all recognition and are for the most part in a poor state of repair. I sincerely hope that my descriptions and illustrations will bring back happy memories to many local people, and that this publication will also be helpful to students of both the history and the architecture of Hull during the Victorian era.

Two buildings greatly impressed me when I was very young, namely the former Hammond's store and Beverley Minster, said to be the finest Gothic church in Europe. These later led to my desire to study architecture.

Although Street's All Saints', Margaret Street, was said to set the standard for many of the churches built in Hull about this time, it did not in any way compare with Butterfield's famous All Saints' in Margaret Street, London, which I know well. Nevertheless, I had a special affection for a number of churches which we have lost: St Mark's, Groves; St Stephen's, off Hessle Road; St Augustine's, Princes Avenue; St Nicholas', Pickering Park; and the great Jubilee chapel on Spring Bank. Sadly, most of the other churches and chapels described have long since been demolished and in a few instances new smaller buildings of little architectural significance have been erected in their place. However, it is heartening to note that at the present time much restoration work is taking place on Hull's two great architectural treasures, namely Holy Trinity and St Mary's Lowgate churches.

I now feel that I was rather unkind about the Law Courts section of the Guildhall facing Alfred Gelder Street. What a pity that the city fathers of the time did not see fit to keep Brodrick's Town Hall and link it to the Law Courts with a carefully designed first-floor bridge, on the lines of that made between Waterhouse's famous Manchester Town Hall and the Town Hall Extension.

During the last 50 years many important changes for the better have been made in Hull, including the redesign of Queen's Gardens in the 1960s and the building of the Clive Sullivan Way after the completion of the Humber Bridge. This together with the improvement of Castle Street and the new bridge over the River Hull enabled a large section of the city centre to be pedestrianised and the Old Town area to be revitalised to include new housing. The establishment of the Marina in the town docks, the conversion of old warehouses, and the Princes Quay development have led to more people living in the centre of the city. The new buildings that have been slotted in between those that remained in High Street after the Second World War are also praiseworthy.

Although much still remains to be done in certain areas, the centre of the city for the most part is now very attractive.

IAN GOLDTHORPE
Grassington, June 2005

INTRODUCTION

The destruction already wrought by two wars has been responsible for the complete loss of a number of the finest buildings erected in Hull during the Victorian period. Many more buildings were seriously damaged, and their shells in many cases still stood in 1955 as stark reminders of the grim days of war; most were too badly damaged to be repaired, and were due for demolition. Other buildings were later removed to make way for road widening and improvements, and slum clearance schemes led to the demolition of many churches and schools which, despite architectural interest, were considered to be redundant or obsolete.

Rapid industrial expansion and the general movement of residential areas to the outskirts have also greatly changed the use of many parts of the city. Houses have been bought and pulled down to make room for rapidly expanding factories; many churches, chapels and other once important buildings have likewise been used to house the requirements of industry.

Hull produced a number of architects of outstanding ability during the period, of whom some achieved more than local fame. Other buildings were the subject of architectural competitions and were designed by various well-known architects of the time.

Many beautiful buildings still remained in 1955, either in their complete state or in ruins, but at that time it was evident that many buildings would soon be gone forever. It was for this reason that I decided to devote my thesis to the architecture of the Victorian era in Kingston upon Hull, in a survey of the principal buildings erected in the city between 1830 and 1914.

No writer had at that time undertaken a study of the Victorian architecture of Hull, and the most recently published history was still that written by Joseph Sheahan in 1866. More concerned with the development of the city as a whole, Sheahan only commented upon buildings and architectural schemes of outstanding importance.

The term Victorian is here used to describe the architecture of the period from about 1830 up to the beginning of the First World War. In fact the great series of architectural revivals, known today as Victorian architecture, had begun even earlier. The early Gothic Revival showed its first signs in Hull as early as 1822, when St Peter's church, Drypool was rebuilt and Christ Church was erected. This was followed in 1828 by the first important building in the style of the early Classical Revival.

By 1830 only four buildings of importance had been built in the new styles, with no noticeable effect on the appearance of the town. 1830, however, marked a significant change. After this date houses with red brick façades and Georgian doorways gave way to houses with stuccoed façades, windows with few glazing bars and projecting porticoes. These were usually of the Greek revival and public buildings likewise began to be designed in the same style. In 1830 St James's church was the first building of prime importance to be erected in Hull in the style of the early Gothic Revival.

The main aims of this study are to trace the development of architectural styles and influences through the period, and to study and compare the buildings of each architectural era. The story is complex as different styles and influences operated simultaneously in the architecture of the town. Chapter II traces the development of Hull from c.1830 to 1914 through the work of its leading architects, and forms a background to the subsequent chapters which will deal with the individual architectural periods. Chapter I provides an introduction to the subject, and describes briefly the architectural and historical development of the town from its foundation.

In 1955, only a small number of buildings of this period were scheduled for preservation under the Ancient Monuments Act and, with few exceptions, these buildings were all erected before 1850.

During recent years much more interest has been shown in attempting to understand the complex architecture of the Victorian era. A number of recent books have also been published, concerned mainly with the work of the more important architects of the period.

Many buildings of this period were not very comfortable places in which to live and work. Some were examples of bad or tight planning behind elaborate, exciting and sometimes comical façades. Windows were not always suited to function and often produced dark and uninspiring interiors. Many buildings have since undergone drastic internal alterations which have often completely destroyed the original design.

The development of the many slum areas during this period has undeservedly given the era as a whole a bad name. However, many buildings of great architectural beauty, and displaying a high standard of craftsmanship, were also erected in this period.

It is heartening to see that an ever-increasing number of people are beginning to realise the tremendous achievements of our Victorian architects. It was, indeed, an age of prosperity and building such as had never been seen before and may never occur again.

CONTENTS

LIST OF PLATES

LIST OF ILLUSTRATIONS

CHAPTER I

THE EARLY HISTORY AND GROWTH OF THE TOWN

Kingston upon Hull, a medieval seaport which developed under royal ownership, grew up on the banks of the river Hull where it joins the Humber. Situated twenty miles from the open sea, with over seven miles of docks and quays, it became one of the principal seaports of the United Kingdom, one of the world's leading fishing ports and a flourishing centre of trade and industry.

In the earliest references the town was named Wyke, a name whose origin is obscure. There are many conjectures as to its meaning, amongst them 'a refuge', 'a retreat', 'the entrance to a river', or just simply 'the village'. Wyke does not appear in the Domesday Book, for at that time it formed only a parcel of the township of Myton, which is included as a berewick of the manor of Ferriby.

In the 12th century Wyke and Myton fell largely into the hands of Meaux Abbey, founded in 1150 by William, Earl of Albemarle. In 1160 Maud de Camin sold a portion of Wyke to the monks of Meaux; further property in the town was conveyed to Meaux Abbey in 1174. Wyke at this time lay partly in the parish of Hessle and partly in that of Ferriby. A church was built on the site of the present Holy Trinity church (1) before 1160 as a chapel of ease to Hessle church, serving those parishioners who were at times resident in Wyke. It was a very simple structure and was destroyed by fire during a quarrel between the monks of Meaux Abbey and the vicar of Hessle.

By the late 13th century the town was developing as a centre for trade. In 1278 the Abbot of Meaux successfully petitioned for the right to hold a market on Thursday of each week and an annual fair, and in 1281-2 Wyke was the fourth port in England for the export of wool. Its development was favoured by the demise of Ravenserodd, closer to the mouth of the Humber, which began to suffer from erosion at this time, and by the intervention of the King. In 1293 Edward I acquired all the property of the Abbey of Meaux in Wyke and Myton, and on 1 April 1299 he granted the town its first charter as the free borough of Kingston upon Hull.

Together with many other royal privileges, the charter granted the right to hold two markets a week, on Tuesday and Friday, and one fair every year. In 1302 authority was given to build roads linking Hull with Holderness, Beverley and Hessle via Anlaby. The straight main roads then planned have continued in use to the present day and constitute the principal framework of the contemporary road system. The importance of the new borough is further illustrated by the establishment in March 1300 of a mint. Over time many more privileges were bestowed on the town

and in 1440 a charter of incorporation was granted; at the same time the town was made a county in itself, separate from the County of York.

There has been considerable difference of opinion as to the size of the town at the end of the 13th century. It is now thought that the town had become an important transhipment port but was still quite small with probably fewer than 2,000 inhabitants. The Royal Tilery (to the west of the town) was in production by 1304, and the de la Poles opened a second one (to the north) which was in operation by 1320. The town walls were constructed from bricks produced at these yards.

Holy Trinity church (1) is the only building standing in the town today which dates from the days of Edward I. Although not completed in his time, there is little doubt that the work was carried out on the lines originally planned. Holy Trinity is one of the largest parish churches in the country. Its size and massive proportions show the great importance Edward attached to the new foundation; this church was indeed intended to serve a great town, a role it still plays today. A second church had been built on the site of that destroyed earlier. However, in less than 100 years this building had become inadequate, and the foundations of the present church were laid about 1285. The new church was built while the old one was still standing, and the arch between the north transept and the north choir aisle is all that now remains of the second church. The south transept was the first part of the present church to be built, and was followed by the choir, north transept and lower part of the tower, all in the curvilinear Decorated style. These sections of the church were built in brick, with stone used only for the windows, parapets, pinnacles and quoins of the buttresses, and it is today one of the oldest brick buildings in the country. The work was brought to a standstill in the 1340s by the Black Death. After a long delay building began again and the church was completed and consecrated on 10 March 1425.

Holy Trinity measures 285 feet from east to west and nearly 100 feet along the transepts. The roof of the nave is over 70 feet above the floor of the church and the central tower (3) rises to 150 feet. The building is remarkable for its light and delicate construction, made necessary by the poor bearing pressure of the subsoil. The foundations of the central tower rest on huge timber rafts designed to spread the load as much as possible. The large windows, designed to reduce the weight of the structure, make the interior of the church a lantern of light (2). The church narrowly escaped destruction when in two world wars it was scarred

1 – Holy Trinity Church – View from the East

2 – South Choir Aisle

3 – Central Tower

4 – Statue of King William III

by bomb and blast, which razed to the ground buildings which stood only a few yards away, and still stands majestically above its surroundings (1).

St Mary's, Lowgate (XI), is first mentioned in 1327 in the will of William Skayll and was founded as a chapel of ease of North Ferriby. A considerable amount of building took place in the 14th and 15th centuries. There is an apocryphal story that Henry VIII caused the steeple and a large part of the body of the church to be removed when he enlarged Suffolk Palace, which he had acquired from the de la Poles, and that some of the materials thereby obtained were also used for the erection of the blockhouses on Garrison Side, to the east of the river Hull. In 1518 the west end of St Mary's 'fell entirely down'. The chancel was left in a forlorn state until about 1588 when three new bays were added to the east end. This new work is noticeable since the arches are much lighter than those of the older part of the church. In 1696 the foundation of a new steeple was laid and it was completed in the following year. The illustration of the church in 1790 (XI) shows the building much as it would have appeared immediately after the completion of the tower. The steeple and part of the south aisle were constructed substantially of brick, with stone used only for buttresses, parapets and windows. The remains of a clerestory window are clearly visible at the western end, adjoining the steeple.

At the Reformation the townspeople petitioned Parliament for the separation of their churches from the mother parishes. Holy Trinity was separated from Hessle in 1661, but St Mary's was not declared a parish until 1868.

High Street was soon developed by the wealthy merchants and was the part of the town where they lived and worked. Wilberforce House (5) was the finest, and is today one of the few remaining, merchants' houses. It was once thought that it was built about 1590 by Sir John Lister and that in 1639 he entertained Charles I there, but it is now considered that the house dates from the 1660s. The house later passed into the hands of the Wilberforce family and here William Wilberforce was born, the most famous of all Hull men.

One old building still remaining in the city from early times is the Olde White Harte in Silver Street. In 1642 Sir John Hotham, Governor of Hull, refused Charles I admittance to the town, and the 'Plotting Parlour' in the Olde White Harte, in which he is reputed to have made this decision, may still be seen. It is now thought that the inn dates from the 1660s, but there is always the possibility that an earlier building existed on the site.

Another ancient building is the Grammar School, which was founded in 1486 by John Alcock, who in turn became Bishop of Rochester, Worcester and Ely. In 1583 the old structure was in a ruinous state and Alderman William Gee opened a subscription for the rebuilding, himself subscribing £80 and 20,000 bricks for the purpose. The Corporation joined in the work and as a result a second storey was added to the building, which was used as a merchants' exchange and assembly room. The building, which is now a museum, stands on the south side of Holy Trinity church and is constructed of locally manufactured bricks. The building has four-light windows with brick mullions. Between those of the lower storey are three stones bearing the initial 'G', the date 1583 and a curious merchant's mark. Another stone with the same mark and the initials 'W G', bearing the date 1585, probably indicates the year in which the building was finished.

The Charterhouse, situated in what is now Charterhouse Lane (10, 11), was founded in 1384 by Sir Michael de la Pole. Although the Charterhouse was dissolved at the Reformation, it was subsequently refounded.

Hollar's fine engraving of Hull (I) shows that c.1640 there was still quite a lot of space left for building within the walls of the town. The most densely built-up area is between the river and the High Street, where the houses of the merchants can clearly be seen. Wilberforce House, the sixth house to the south of Salter Staithe, is clearly the largest house in the street. Suffolk Palace is shown with a tower, and St Mary's church has a north aisle but no steeple. Holy Trinity church is shown much as it is today, and the Grammar School is also indicated to the south-west of Holy Trinity. The layout of the streets is largely the same as today (II) and the town is completely surrounded by water, on the east and south sides by the rivers, and on the west and north sides by a moat. On the eastern side of the river the blockhouses can be seen and beyond these the ancient church at Drypool. One bridge is shown linking the two sides of the river Hull.

4 December 1734 saw the inauguration of the equestrian statue of King William III (4) in the Market Place. Designed and executed by Peter Scheemakers, it was erected by public subscription at a cost of £893.

The foundation of Trinity House (6, 9) dates from 1369, when the guild of Holy Trinity was founded by some 30 people. This was not at first a maritime guild but about 1457 amalgamated with the shipmen's guild. In 1521 Henry VIII incorporated a certain number of the brethren, and empowered them to purchase lands and tenements to the amount of ten pounds a year. Thomas Ferres, an Elder Brother and three times Warden, was the principal benefactor of this institution, purchasing the site of the monastery of the Whitefriars, situated on the south side of the modern Whitefriargate.

The almshouse facing White Friars' Lane (6) was rebuilt in 1753 and about this time the road was renamed Trinity House Lane. The design for the rebuilding of Trinity House (6, 9) is usually attributed to Jeremiah Hargrave, and the building itself, which is of brick with a stuccoed front, is in the Tuscan style. In plan it consists of four sides

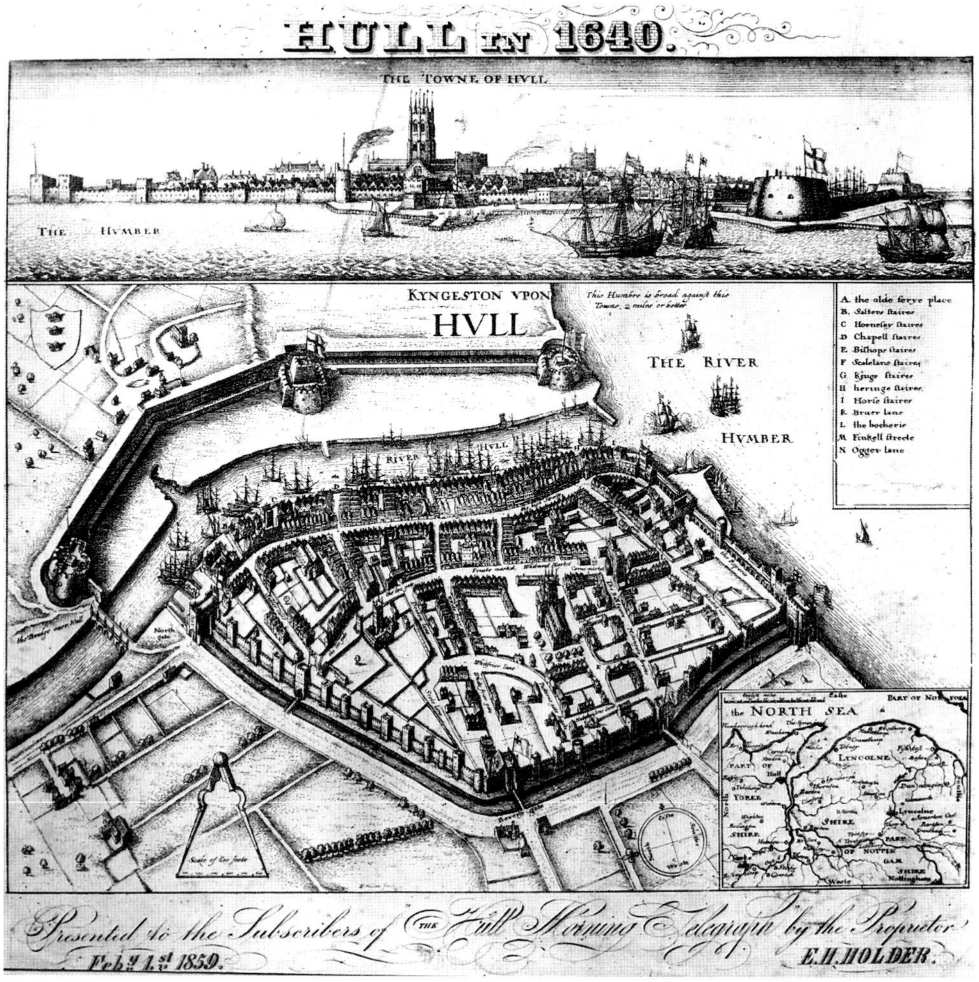

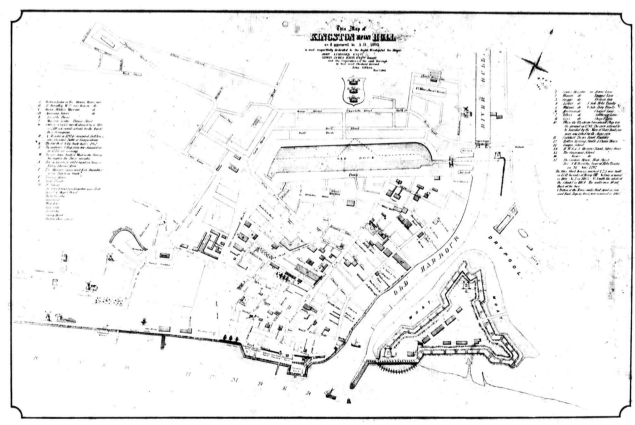

PLATE I – Hollar's Plan of Kingston upon Hull, 1640

PLATE II – J. Aitken's Map of Kingston upon Hull, 1800

5 – WILBERFORCE HOUSE

6 – TRINITY HOUSE

7 – GENERAL INFIRMARY – MAIN STAIRCASE

8 – NEPTUNE INN, WHITEFRIARGATE

surrounding a spacious courtyard, three sides of which contain 30 rooms for Younger Brethren and master mariners' widows. The front of the building has rustic stone quoins, a stone plinth, stone architraves to the windows and a stone cornice. The pediment is entirely of freestone, with a large carving of the Royal Arms supported by figures of Neptune and Britannia, by Jeremiah Hargrave.

A few years later the eminent London-based architect, Sir William Chambers, was engaged to design the courthouse and chapel adjoining the almshouses in Trinity House Lane; these buildings, which occupied the site immediately to the north of the almshouses, have since been pulled down. Sir William Chambers was probably employed either for his eminence or on account of some connection with the port through his father's business.

About this time the ditches which protected the walls of the town were partly filled in, and sections of the walls themselves were pulled down. Trade was expanding and the harbour formed by the river Hull soon became inadequate for the number of ships using the port. In 1773 Hull Dock Company was formed and was granted the walls, ramparts and ditches on the north and west sides of the town. In 1775 the first stone of the first dock was laid by the Mayor, and in 1778 the new dock, later Queen's Dock, was opened. Following this development, Hull began to extend beyond the confines of the original town.

The new Charterhouse buildings, in Charterhouse Lane, were rebuilt in their present form 1778-80, probably to the designs of Joseph Hargrave. The Master's House was extensively rebuilt after bomb damage in the Second World War, and there have since been additions to the main block. The front buildings (10, 11), which are of brick and two storeys high, comprise a centre block flanked by projecting wings with another range behind. The entrance to the hospital comprises a semi-circular portico supported by six Tuscan columns, with an architrave bearing the inscription:

DEO & PAUPERIBUS, MICHAEL DE LA POLE,
COMES DE SUFFOLK, HAS AEDES POSUIT A.D. MCCCLXXXIIII
RENOVATAS ITERUM AUCTIUSQUE INSTAURATAS PIAE
FUNDATORIS MEMORIAE
D.D. JOHANNAS BOURNE RECTOR AD. MDCCLXXX

Within the tympanum of the pediment above the door are the de la Pole arms. On the summit of the roof there is a circular cupola consisting of eight Ionic columns supporting a dome.

In October 1781 Hull General Infirmary was founded, and a subscription was started for erecting and supporting this house of mercy. A temporary establishment was opened in September 1782, and in the meantime two acres of land on the outskirts of the town were purchased at a cost of £550. It was decided to hold a competition for the design of a suitable building, with a premium of 20 guineas.

9 – TRINITY HOUSE – ENTRANCE

10 – CHARTER-HOUSE – PORTICO

11 – CHARTER-HOUSE – CENTRAL BLOCK

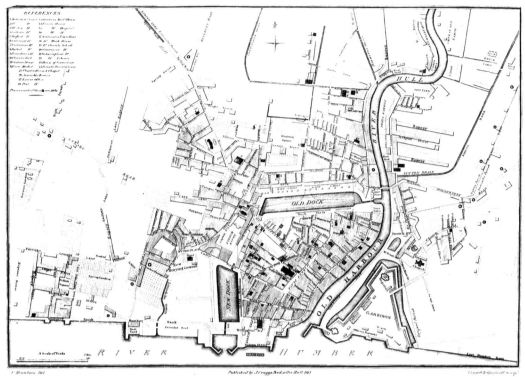

PLATE III – J. Cragg's Plan of Kingston upon Hull, 1817

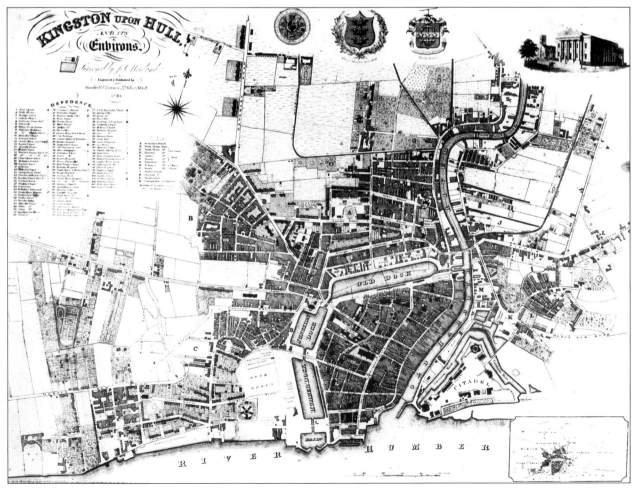

PLATE IV – Goodwill & Lawson's Plan of Kingston upon Hull, 1834

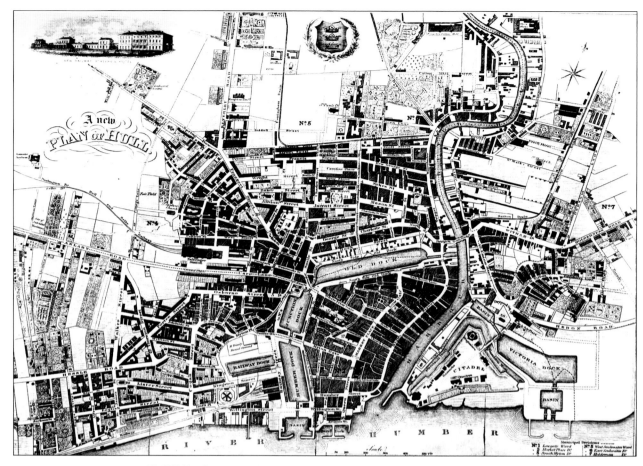

PLATE V – Goodwill & Lawson's Plan of Kingston upon Hull, 1850

PLATE VI – Goodwill & Lawson's Plan of Kingston upon Hull, 1857

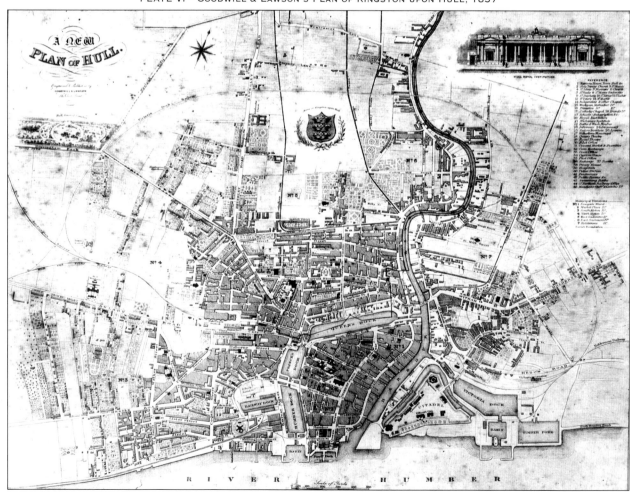

The design submitted by George Pycock of Lowgate, Hull, was selected as the most suitable and he was awarded the prize.

Pycock's design (XII) was simple but very effective. The main entrance was approached by a flight of steps and above, on the first floor, was a Palladian window. The building was erected in 1784 at a cost of c.£4,000 and formed the nucleus of the Royal Infirmary in Prospect Street, now demolished. Although the front had been altered by 1955, much of Pycock's work could still be seen from the back, and his main staircase (7) remained in its original simple form. George Pycock is regarded as one of the earliest known architects in Hull, though Joseph Page, designer of Maister's House, preceded him.

In 1784 George Pycock won a competition for the design of a gaol in Mytongate, and in 1794 he designed the Neptune Inn in Whitefriargate (8) for the Corporation of Trinity House. George Pycock, although initially a builder, became a local architect of great distinction and was responsible for the three most important buildings erected in Hull in the latter part of the 18th century, before reputedly retiring to Malton.

The Neptune Inn was considered to be the best of his works, and at that time was one of the finest hostelries in the north of England. The fine archway on the front gave access to a spacious courtyard surrounded by buildings and stables. This building was later used as the Custom House and, when vacated by the Customs in 1908, became known as Custom House Buildings. In recent years the ground floor has been converted into shops, but the entrance archway and fine façade above remain unchanged.

To create a route from the Old Town to the dock, Parliament Street (12) was built, affording a fine view from the windows of the Neptune Inn. The Corporation of Trinity House were invited to contribute to the cost but declined in view of the heavy expense of the Neptune Inn. However, by 1796, a large sum of money had been raised and the subscribers obtained an Act of Parliament for laying out and making the new street. Parliament Street was laid out by Charles Mountain senior and Thomas Riddell, who were probably also responsible for the design and construction of the houses. This was the second attempt in Hull to produce a well-designed street. Land of Green Ginger, whose name had been changed from Old Beverley Street c.1830, was originally intended to form a fine crescent.

Charles Mountain was a contemporary of the Pycocks who traded as a builder from Princes Street in 1791 and later from Myton Place. He probably designed the Minerva Lodge, Princes Street, in 1802. His son Charles Mountain junior also became an important Hull architect.

Following the opening of the first dock in 1778, the Hull Dock Company started to develop land to

12 – HOUSES – PARLIAMENT STREET

13 – HOUSES – CHARLOTTE STREET

14 – DOCK OFFICE

15 – PILOT OFFICE

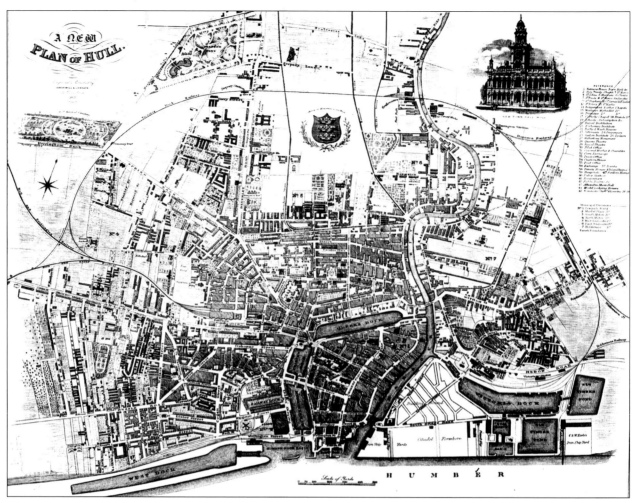

PLATE VII – GOODWILL & LAWSON'S PLAN OF KINGSTON UPON HULL, 1869

PLATE VIII – M. C. PECK'S PLAN OF KINGSTON UPON HULL, 1875

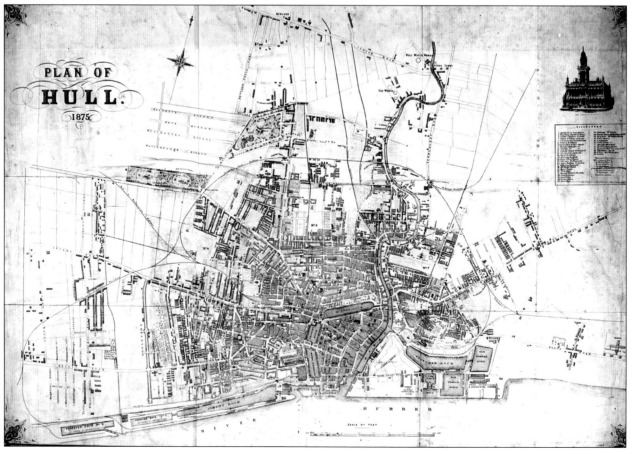

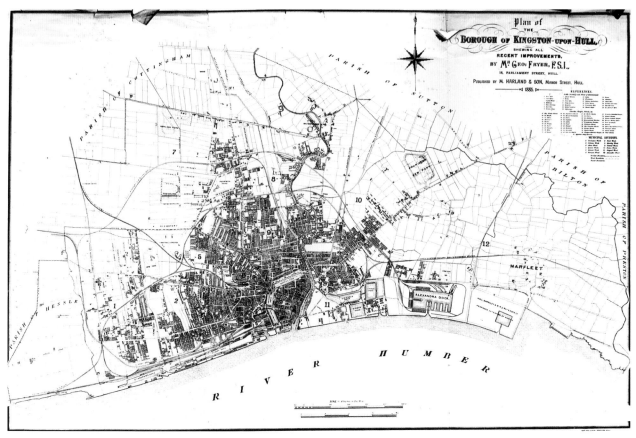

PLATE IX – G. FRYER'S PLAN OF KINGSTON UPON HULL, 1885

PLATE X – BACON'S PLAN OF KINGSTON UPON HULL, 1908

PLATE XI – St Mary's Church, Lowgate, 1790

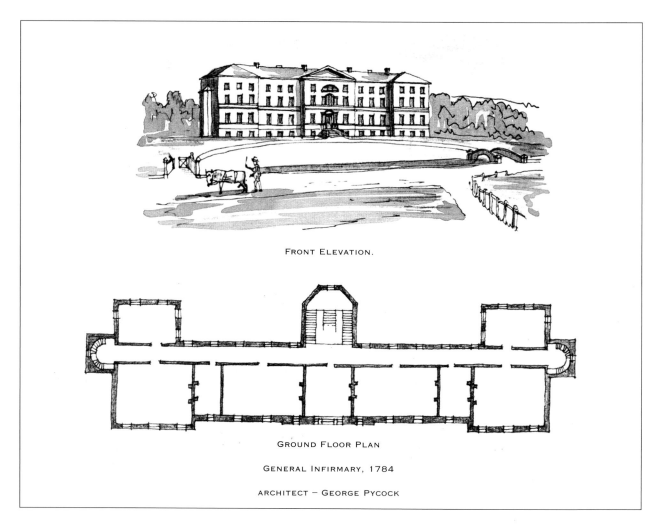

Front Elevation.

Ground Floor Plan

General Infirmary, 1784

ARCHITECT – George Pycock

PLATE XII – General Infirmary, 1784

the north and west. Bower's plan of 1791 shows that by then a considerable amount of development had been undertaken in this area. The streets laid out by the Dock Company were Savile Street, George Street, Charlotte Street and North Street. The development in Savile Street was very poor, but George Street and Charlotte Street (13) were much more imposing. The dock surveyor, Mr Holt, is said to have laid out the streets, and the houses were built to the design of Charles Mountain senior by, amongst others, Edward and Thomas Riddell.

About 1790 the area between Savile Street and Beverley Road was purchased by Richard Baker, who was a very wealthy man. He laid out Albion Street and Baker Street, and Edward Story built Story Street. Albion Street is the best example of development in this area, since from the outset it was intended for housing of first-class quality. The Albion Street houses (16), although designed for individual clients, present a continuous façade with a common eaves line.

The first church to be built outside the Old Town was the church of St John in St John's Street at the western end of Whitefriargate. It was erected in 1791 at a cost of £4,600 and was pulled down to make way for the Ferens Art Gallery.

As a result of the development outside the Old Town area, Prospect Street, which had formed a link between Whitefriargate and the road to Beverley, was cut off by the Savile Street, Chariot Street and Waterworks Street development.

At the end of the 18th century the growth of the town beyond the medieval walls was confined to the Prospect Street area, the area north of the dock and the area to the west of the Old Town, from Carr Lane to the Humber. Aitken's map of Hull (II) shows the town as it appeared in 1800 and the extent of new development outside the Old Town area.

The trade of the port continued to expand and it was soon necessary to provide additional accommodation for ships. In 1809 a second dock was opened, known later as Humber Dock and today as the Marina. The first dock was then known as 'Old Dock', and the second was referred to as 'New Dock'.

Cragg's Map of 1817 (III) shows Jarratt Street and Kingston Square, which were laid out in 1810. By 1820 the first buildings were erected in Kingston Square. A northward extension of High

16 – HOUSES – ALBION STREET

17 – HOUSES – SPRING STREET

18 – ST CHARLES'S CHURCH, JARRATT STREET

Street is shown to form Wincolmlee and is interesting since it follows almost exactly the bends of the river Hull. There was also an attempt to form a main road running almost due north from George Street, known as Grimston Street. It was later extended to form Worship Street and then continued to become Caroline Street, but Cottingham Drain cut across its path and prevented further development.

Anlaby Road is shown by Cragg as an extension to Carr Lane, and Spring Street was originally intended to link Spring Bank and Anlaby Road. The houses in Spring Street (17), which have now been demolished, were of a much better quality than many others erected at the time. Henry Blundell's brush and paint factory is also shown at the junction of Spring Bank and Beverley Road. This was one of Hull's earliest factories. Certain development had taken place on the east side of the river Hull, but since the only link was by a small bridge, called North Bridge, development was centred mainly around the village of Drypool.

In 1820 the Dock Office (14), the second to be built in Hull, was erected at the eastern end of Old Dock. It is an attractive little building with a fine entrance consisting of four Tuscan columns supporting an entablature in the Grecian style. On the roof over the pediment is an elegant lantern with six columns supporting a cupola. Three years later the Pilot Office (15) was erected in Nelson Street. It had a similar entrance to the Dock Office and was interesting for its curved lookout window on the top floor. The entrance has since been moved. The original entrance was round the corner in Nelson Street.

The town had grown considerably since the opening of the first dock in 1778. The map by Goodwill and Lawson (IV) shows the extent of development by about 1830.

19 – WILBERFORCE MONUMENT

19A – MODEL OF GREAT THORNTON STREET CHAPEL

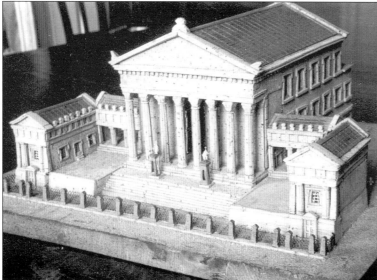

CHAPTER II

THE GROWTH OF THE CITY BETWEEN 1830 AND 1914

Pre-1850

This chapter examines the growth of the city during the Victorian era and the architects responsible for the more important and interesting buildings erected at that time. Subsequent chapters will concentrate on the buildings themselves. Although Kingston Square was laid out in 1801, it was not until 1822 that the first building of importance was erected there. This was Christ Church (44), which has now been demolished apart from the former church hall (originally Christ Church Schools, designed 1847-9 by Cuthbert Brodrick). It was sited to the north-east of Kingston Square in John Street and the architect was William Hutchinson.

WILLIAM HUTCHINSON (1779-1869) is first mentioned in the 1806 Hull directory, where he is described as a house carpenter and builder who lived in George Yard. In the 1821 directory he is described as an architect and builder, at the same address. Later directories classify him as an architect and he continued in practice until about 1840. Charles Hutchinson, who was probably his son, then continued the practice from the same address until 1855.

William Hutchinson was essentially a builder-architect of the early Gothic Revival, and his main commissions were for the design of churches. In 1822 the new churches of St Peter, Drypool (43), now demolished, and Christ Church, Kingston Square (44) were erected to his designs. In 1833 he designed St John's, Newland (318).

In 1829 the Roman Catholic church of St Charles Borromeo was completed in Jarratt Street, situated on the south side of Kingston Square. The front of the building (18) is in the Florentine style. The interior was originally finished in the Grecian style, but in the late 1890s the aisles were added and the interior was completely remodelled by Immenkamp. John Earle junior was the architect of the original building, which was widened and altered internally and externally by J. J. Scoles in 1835.

JOSEPH JOHN SCOLES (1798-1864) was articled in 1812 to Joseph Ireland (1780-1841), a leading Roman Catholic architect of the day. Scoles began to practise in 1819 and travelled from 1822 to 1826. St Charles's, Hull, was one of his first commissions after returning from his travels. He designed many Roman Catholic churches and in 1831 began St Peter's, Great Yarmouth. He also designed churches at Edgbaston and at Southtown, Great Yarmouth. His pupil S. J. Nickoll completed some of his later works.

The next building of importance to be erected in Kingston Square was the Assembly Rooms, now the New Theatre (XIII). The building is situated on the east side of the square, a site thought to have been chosen on account of its proximity to Sculcoates Town Hall, which was situated immediately to the east. The building is in the Grecian style and was designed by Charles Mountain, a prominent local architect of the time.

CHARLES MOUNTAIN junior (1773-1839) was the son of Charles Mountain, the builder-architect of the late 18th century. Charles Mountain junior designed the Theatre Royal, Humber Street, in 1809 and first appears in the Hull directory for 1814, where he is described as an architect practising from 22 Portland Place; from 1817 to 1831 he worked from 59 Prospect Street.

In the early days his commissions were mainly small, and he is thought to have been responsible for a good number of houses in the town, although there is no direct evidence identifying the houses he designed. No. 215 Anlaby Road (39) includes an entrance portico in the Doric order, which was Mountain's favourite style, but dates from the early 1840s and is more probably by George Jackson. Another house in Coleridge Street, east of the river Hull, has similar proportions, and a similar Doric entrance portico, but has suffered considerably from later alterations.

Charles Mountain was appointed as architect to Hull Trinity House c.1825 and from then on undertook a number of commissions of a more civic nature. In 1826 he designed the almshouses in Posterngate (XIII) and in 1829-30 he designed a property on the south side of Whitefriargate adjoining the Neptune Inn (20) for Smith's Bank, which is adorned by a sculptured tympanum executed by a local sculptor, Thomas Earle.

In 1830 Mountain designed the Mechanics' Institute in Charlotte Street, and the Assembly Rooms in Kingston Square. About this time he also worked on the Town Hall at Beverley. His last building was the Master Mariners' Almshouse in Carr Lane (XIII) which was built in 1834. Following the completion of this building, Mountain retired to Malton.

1834 marked the erection of the monument in memory of William Wilberforce (19) at the western end of Whitefriargate. The architect responsible for the design and supervision of the work was John Clark of Leeds.

THOMAS EARLE (1810-76), the celebrated local sculptor, was born in Osborne Street, Hull, in 1810. In very early life he showed a talent for modelling, and at the age of 12 may be said to have commenced

20 – SMITH'S BANK, WHITEFRIARGATE

21 – POSTERNGATE ALMSHOUSE

24 – SCHOOL OF ANATOMY AND MEDICINE, KINGSTON SQUARE

22 – OCEANUS BY THOMAS EARLE

23 – ASSEMBLY ROOMS, KINGSTON SQUARE

his career as a sculptor. In 1830 he left his native town for London and was shortly afterwards engaged by Sir Francis Chantrey as an assistant. Here he remained for eight years, modelling and working upon many of that eminent sculptor's best productions. During this time he studied at the Royal Academy and in 1839 gained the gold medal and other honours. Hull is rich in well-known works of this talented townsman, chief among them the statue of Queen Victoria (191) in Pearson Park. The figure of Oceanus (22) over the Posterngate almshouses (now in front of Trinity House Chapel), and the river gods of the Smith's Bank tympanum in Whitefriargate (20) are excellent examples of his early work. The fine sculptured group in the tympanum of the building at the south-west corner of Parliament Street (now demolished) was another.

Following Mountain's retirement, H. R. Abraham of London was employed to complete the Assembly Rooms. Abraham had married a sister of Richard Bethell, of Rise, and it was through Bethell's influence that he obtained this commission.

H. R. ABRAHAM (1803/04-1877) was the son of Robert Abraham (1775-1850), a noted architect. He designed the Hull School of Anatomy and Medicine in Kingston Square, of which only the façade remains today, incorporated in a new block of apartments (24).

In 1829 Junction Dock was opened, completing the dock system and once more surrounding the Old Town with water. Following the opening of Junction Dock, New Dock became known as Humber Dock. Goodwill and Lawson's map of 1834 (IV) shows the completed system of docks, but development remained sparse. As Carr Lane only began to develop c.1835 it was mainly confined to filling in the area to the south of Osborne Street.

The Botanic Gardens, which were opened in 1812 off Anlaby Road, at the end of what became Linnaeus Street, are first shown on Cragg's map of 1817 (III). On the 1834 map (IV) they appear well laid out with trees and paths. Linnaeus Street was not built up by this time, although a number of houses, good examples of the Grecian Revival with a late Regency air about them, had already been erected on Anlaby Road.

By 1834 all the main roads had been established, and it is interesting to note that, with the exception of Beverley and Hedon Roads, all run directly on the line of Holy Trinity church tower. The map of this date (IV) shows that a number of houses had already been erected on the west side of Beverley Road (42). Several houses in various parts of the town, including Lister Street, have the same window heads and are probably the work of the same builder, although the Beverley Road houses are of a much higher quality.

Lister Street to the south of Hessle Road was laid out c.1829 with St James's Square at its western end (IV). Lister Street is Hull's first example of a street laid out with a church as its focal point. This area quickly developed as a popular residential neighbourhood among the more wealthy citizens of the merchant and tradesman type. Its main attractions were the pleasant walks available at this time along the Humber bank, and an area marked 'Intended Terrace' is shown on the 1834 map (IV).

Soon after the completion of St James's church, houses began to appear in Lister Street with small front and large rear gardens. No attempt was made to maintain a uniform eaves line, and the result was not nearly so successful as the Albion Street development. The two houses in Lister Street (XXII) were the finest still standing in 1955, and were reminiscent of many of the town houses of the Regency period. The three houses in St James's Square (XXIII) were of a slightly later date. Both groups of houses, although pleasantly proportioned, were clumsily detailed, and it is unlikely that they were anything more than good-class builders' houses of the time. The Lister Street houses had completely stuccoed façades. Only the pilasters of the St James's Square houses were finished with stucco, the remainder of the façade being faced in brickwork in Flemish bond.

In 1829 the committee for erecting the new St James's church obtained a site of 700 square yards 'at the west end of a large and spacious street to be called Lister Street'. The Commissioners for Building New Churches agreed to pay two-thirds of the cost of the building, and it was subsequently decided to arrange an architectural competition for the design. The plan of the church as built (XXIV), together with the submission of a number of classical designs, strongly suggests that a classical design would have been more suited to the committee's requirements. Charles Mountain junior was among those who submitted a design in a classical style. His design was not accepted, and it is unlikely that he had any other involvement in the development of the area since none of the houses are of a sufficiently high architectural standard.

The design submitted by Messrs Hansom and Welsh of York was adjudged the most suitable and was accepted. The church (47), which was demolished in 1957, was built in 1830 at a cost of about £6,500.

JOSEPH ALOYSIUS HANSOM (1803-82) was articled to Matthew Philips at York. He settled at Halifax and became assistant to a Mr Oates. He later went into partnership with Edward Welsh and designed St James's, Hull; churches at Toxteth Park, Liverpool and Acomb, York; and three in the Isle of Man. From 1854 to 1859 he worked in partnership with his brother Charles Francis; from 1859 to 1861 with his eldest son; and from 1862 to 1863 with Edward Welby Pugin. He also designed many other Roman Catholic churches, but remains better known as the inventor of the Hansom Cab.

In 1836 Kingston College (70) was erected on Beverley Road at a cost of £4,500; originally built in the Tudor style, it has since been altered and is

POSTERNGATE ALMSHOUSE, 1826

ASSEMBLY, KINGSTON SQUARE, 1830

MASTER MARINERS' ALMSHOUSE, CARR LANE, 1834

PLATE XIII – THREE BUILDINGS DESIGNED BY CHARLES MOUNTAIN JUNIOR

now Kingston Youth Centre. The architect was H. F. Lockwood who had recently started to practise in Hull.

HENRY FRANCIS LOCKWOOD, FSA (1811-78) was born at Doncaster and when still quite young went to York, where he served his articles. He was a keen student of Gothic architecture and was probably articled to Messrs Atkinson, who were the leading ecclesiastical architects in York at the time.

Whilst he was in York he became friendly with Adolphus H. Cates, who was probably another architectural student. With Cates he was co-author of *The History and Antiquities of the Fortifications of the City of York*, which was published in January 1834. This comprehensive study demonstrates Lockwood's keen interest in medieval art and is well illustrated by a number of large engravings, most of them Lockwood's work.

Lockwood practised in Hull from 9 Dock Street for 14 years. Shortly after completing his scheme for Kingston College, he designed the British School (XXVII), which was erected in 1838 in Dansom Lane, on the eastern side of the river Hull, and is now much altered. The two buildings shared many similarities in decoration and figure carving.

In 1834, soon after his arrival in Hull, Lockwood was appointed architect to Trinity House, in succession to Charles Mountain. In tune with his time, Lockwood was eclectic, modelling his work on one or other of the historic styles. In 1839 he designed the new chapel for Trinity House (XVI), his first building in the classical style. Great Thornton Street chapel (XVIII), built in 1841 and opened in 1842, has been demolished. With its fine Corinthian portico, it was probably his most able composition and showed his ability to work in almost any historical style. His design for Albion Independent chapel, Albion Street (XIV), erected in 1841, was also distinguished.

Between 1840 and 1843 he produced many of his finest buildings. In 1841 the foundation stone was laid for St Mark's church (XXV), now demolished. In 1842 work started on Holy Trinity church, and the foundation stone of St Stephen's church, also now demolished, was laid (XXVI). The erection of St Stephen's church in St Stephen's Square, together with the layout of St Stephen's Street, provided Hull's second example of a street planned with a church as its focal point. It was not, however, until the late 1850s that St Stephen's Street itself began to be built up.

In 1844 Lockwood designed Sculcoates Union Workhouse, all of which has now been demolished (73-76). One of his last major commissions before he left Hull was the extension of Hull General Infirmary, which he carried out in 1846. He also designed a number of buildings outside Hull, perhaps including the old vicarage at Kirk Ella of 1839.

Lockwood later went into partnership with a Bradford man, William Mawson, and in 1850 moved to Bradford. His partnership with Mawson started another era in his progress. In 1851 they began work on the industrial estate of Saltaire for Sir Titus Salt, who named two streets in commemoration of his architects. They designed many buildings in Bradford, including St George's Hall, the Exchange and the Town Hall.

Together with Mawson, Lockwood worked on two further buildings in Hull. In 1851 they designed Anlaby Road Workhouse (XXX), built in the Italian style, but demolished to make way for the new Hull Royal Infirmary, and 1878-9 a building at the corner of Whitefriargate and Parliament Street, formerly the Yorkshire Banking Company building, now the HSBC Bank (84). Lockwood and Mawson also designed the City Temple in London. Lockwood served in the Franco-Prussian War and finally retired to the Channel Islands.

Goodwill and Lawson's map of 1834 (IV) shows that the area to the north of Old Dock had grown rapidly and had reached its limit, bounded on the north by Cottingham Drain and on the east by the river Hull. Wincolmlee was as yet the only road which crossed the drain. In 1837 Kingston Flax and Cotton Mills were erected to the north of Cottingham Drain (see the 1850 map by Goodwill and Lawson (V)). The cotton mills, then the largest in the town, employed a considerable number of people living in the area known as 'The Groves', which became notorious for its poor housing. The population increased and the area saw rapid development. Between 1800 and 1840 the town more than doubled its size on the foundation of its prosperous dock system. But the system of large open land drains confined the outward development of the town into clearly defined pockets.

In 1840 the Hull and Selby Railway was opened and a passenger station erected in Kingston Street, to the west of Humber Dock. However, the site of the station proved inconvenient for the town as a whole and, within a few months of its opening, a further line was constructed as a branch to a more conveniently situated passenger station. Owing to the lag in development around Carr Lane an excellent site for a passenger station was available, and the new station in the Italianate style, situated at the western end of Paragon Street, was opened in 1847. The fine hotel, in the same style, was opened in 1851. The architect of both station and hotel was G. T. Andrews of York. Queen Victoria stayed at the hotel in 1854, after which it was renamed the Royal Station Hotel. Also in honour of the Queen's visit, when she circumnavigated Hull, Old Dock was renamed Queen's Dock and Junction Dock was renamed Prince's Dock.

The Kingston Street passenger terminal was pulled down in 1858 and a new goods station on Wellington Street (142), much larger than the former passenger terminal, was erected in its place. It was demolished in 1961.

PLATE XIV –
TWO CHURCHES OF THE EARLY
CLASSICAL REVIVAL

KINGSTON WESLEYAN CHAPEL,
WITHAM

ALBION INDEPENDENT CHAPEL,
ALBION STREET

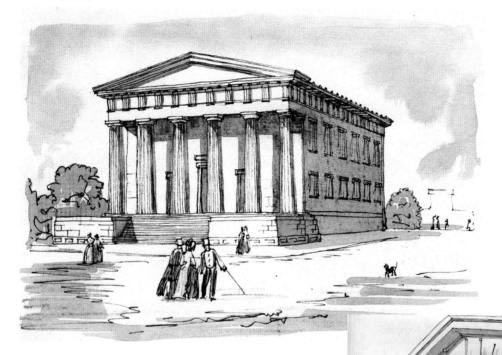

PLATE XV – PORTICO OF THE MASTER MARINERS'
ALMSHOUSE, CARR LANE

In 1846 Railway Dock was opened to the north of Kingston Street on Dock Green (V). A number of warehouses were erected in this area to serve the docks. No. 7 Warehouse in Castle Street (139), between Prince's and Humber Docks, was particularly fine. Erected in 1846, but demolished in 1971, it was designed by John B. Hartley of Liverpool (1814-63), the consulting engineer to the Hull Dock Company 1842-58. He was the son of Jesse Hartley who designed the Liverpool docks and warehouses and was greatly influenced by his father's work. Hartley was also responsible for Railway Dock and Victoria Dock, opened in 1850, now filled in and the site of Victoria Dock Village. Edward Welsh, resident engineer of the Hull Dock Company, also contributed to the development of the area with No. 6 Warehouse, Castle Street (in conjunction with Hartley), opened in 1846, and now restored for commercial use, and No. 13 Warehouse, Railway Dock, opened in 1857 and now the headquarters of the Marina.

The railways spread quickly. In 1846 the Hull and Bridlington line was opened, and in 1854 the Withernsea line, originally terminating at Victoria Dock station. A branch line from the Hull and Hornsea line towards Victoria Dock meant that Hull became completely surrounded by the railways, and level crossings obstructed the main roads in and out of the town.

In 1844 a portion of the extensive parish of Sculcoates was formed into a distinct parish, for ecclesiastical purposes only, under Sir Robert Peel's New Parishes Act of 1843, which aimed to provide for the growing industrial population. St Paul's was one of the earliest parishes so formed. The foundation stone of the church, in Cannon Street, designed by William Dykes, was laid in 1846 and the building completed in 1847 (48); it was demolished in 1976. At the time Holy Trinity was the only church in the town to cover a greater ground floor area. St Paul's vicarage, designed by Ewan Christian of London, and typical of many of his buildings, was not built until 1863.

EWAN CHRISTIAN (1814-95) was first articled to Matthew Habbershaw and afterwards to a Mr Brown of Norwich. He travelled abroad in 1841-2 and in 1842 set up in practice on his own account. He was responsible for a large number of churches of varying quality. In 1847 he completed the restoration of Scarborough parish church and was appointed its architect. He was architect to the Ecclesiastical Commissioners from 1887 and President of the Royal Institute of British Architects from 1884 to 1886.

The existing cemeteries in the town had by now become overcrowded, and in 1847 the General Cemetery was opened on Spring Bank. The design of its gates and lodges was opened to competition and the scheme submitted by Cuthbert Brodrick, a young Hull architect, was accepted.

CUTHBERT BRODRICK (1822-1905) was the son of a local shipowner. He was articled to Henry Francis Lockwood on 4 January 1837, during which time he sketched and measured the principal Gothic structures in the vicinity of Hull. After completing his articles he remained as an assistant with Lockwood for about a year. In 1844 he visited Europe, where his attention was first drawn to classical schemes in Paris, Venice and Rome. On his return to Hull in 1845 he received an offer of a partnership from Lockwood but declined in favour of opening a practice on his own account.

One of his first designs was for the Royal Flower Pot Hotel in Whitefriargate, now demolished; shortly afterwards he won his first architectural competition for the cemetery gates (XXVIII), also now demolished. His first attempt in a classical manner brought him success when his design for the Royal Institution in Albion Street (XIX), destroyed in the Blitz, was accepted in 1852. This building was indeed the forerunner of his greatest achievement, Leeds Town Hall. The design for Leeds Town Hall was the subject of a competition, and it is interesting to note that Lockwood also submitted an entry which was placed second. Brodrick's fine design for Leeds Town Hall set a new standard in civic architecture which has been scarcely equalled since. Following his success he moved his office to Leeds. In the next few years he designed many buildings of distinction throughout the north of England, including the Wells House, Ilkley; the Grand Hotel, Scarborough; and perhaps the railway station, Withernsea.

His last major work on his own account in Hull was the Town Hall. The design was the subject of a competition set by the Corporation in 1861, with premiums of £100 for first place and £50 for second. About 40 schemes were submitted but the Council could not decide which merited their approval. After some discussion it was decided to submit all the entries to Sir William Tite, the celebrated London architect, who declared in favour of Brodrick's design. Lockwood also entered the competition and, as in the case of Leeds Town Hall, his design was placed second.

Brodrick was no doubt Hull's finest architect and, like Lockwood, was able to impart scale and dignity to his designs. He was fortunate in being articled to Lockwood at a time when Lockwood was producing many of his finest buildings in both the Classical and Gothic Revival styles. Cuthbert Brodrick was one of six architects selected by the Government to furnish designs and estimates for a new National Gallery to be erected in London. He left England for Paris in 1869 and became a painter, exhibiting portraits and landscapes at the Royal Academy and Paris Salon. Cuthbert Brodrick died in 1905 and was buried in Jersey.

In 1851 Clowes Primitive Methodist chapel (XXI) was erected in Jarratt Street, to the design of William Sissons. This building was demolished in 1965 and the site redeveloped.

25 – Trinity House Chapel –
West Front

26 – East Front

27 – Trinity House – Entrance Gateway

29 – Bottom Left
Zion Methodist New
Connexion Chapel,
Beverley Road

28 – bottom Right –
Clowes Chapel,
Jarratt Street

EAST ELEVATION

ARCHITECT: H. F. LOCKWOOD

PLATE XVI – TRINITY HOUSE CHAPEL, 1839

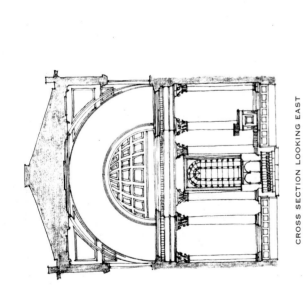

CROSS SECTION LOOKING EAST

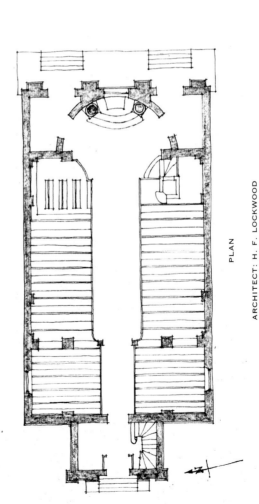

PLAN

ARCHITECT: H. F. LOCKWOOD

PLATE XVII – TRINITY HOUSE CHAPEL, 1839

WILLIAM SISSONS (1833-76) was a Hull architect, builder and surveyor. Sissons was responsible for a number of local buildings: Wesley chapel, Humber Street, 1833; Church Street Primitive Methodist chapel, Wincolmlee, 1846; Great Thornton Street Primitive Methodist chapel, 1849; and Clowes Primitive Methodist chapel, Jarratt Street, 1851. He also designed the Gleadow, Dibb and Co. brewery in Silvester Street, 1867-9. Gleadow, Dibb and Co. became Hull Brewery Company Limited in 1888.

Sissons supervised the construction of George Gilbert Scott's new tower for St Mary's, 1861, and may have designed houses in Albany Street and Cranbourne Street, c.1869. William Sissons, 'land surveyor', certainly drew up a plan of the estate and was a director of the Second Albion Benefit Building Society, its developer. Sissons may also have been responsible for a warehouse on Garrison Side, for E. M. English, 1861, and Malting No. 4, Anlaby Road, for Gleadow, Dibb and Co., 1862.

DAVID THORP (1791-1865) was the first borough surveyor, a post which he held from 1851 until his death. His father, W. Thorp, was a builder. When the North Blockhouse, which stood on the east side of North Bridge, was no longer used for military purposes, it was let in sections to tradesmen. In 1784 his father took the east wing of the building and it was here, in 1791, that David Thorp was born. The blockhouse, however, was pulled down in 1801-2 by order of the Government. David Thorp continued in his father's profession as a builder, from 17 Carlisle Street, and is first mentioned as an architect and surveyor in the 1846 Hull directory.

1850 saw the opening of the baths in Trippett Street (201), now demolished, and the first major building for which he was responsible. In the early 1860s he designed the new Borough Gaol and House of Correction on Hedon Road (79), which was erected 1865-70, but he did not live to see the building started. The foundation stone of the gaol was laid eight days after Thorp died, and R. G. Smith supervised its building. In recent years a single-storey building has been erected across the front of the gaol.

Thorp built the Police Station in Parliament Street, 1853, the Fire Engine House in Edwards Place, Cogan Street, 1863, and the Wool Market (over the Cattle Market) 1865. He also made many manuscript plans of Hull.

RICHARD GEORGE SMITH (c.1837-1901), who succeeded Thorp as borough surveyor, started in practice as an architect and surveyor in Hull c.1855. In 1860 he designed St Charles's Roman Catholic Schools in Pryme Street, and in 1864 he was commissioned to design the new Theatre Royal in Humber Street, on the site of the old building destroyed by fire a few years earlier. That same year he designed the new Humber Lodge in Osborne Street.

In 1865 a competition was held for the design of the proposed Hull and East Riding College to be built in Park Street. Smith submitted a scheme and was successful. The College (77), erected in 1866, was the finest of Smith's earlier buildings.

By 1875 he was in partnership with FREDERICK STEAD BRODRICK (1847-1927), Cuthbert's nephew, and in 1882 they designed St John's, Newington (228). Soon they acquired the services of an assistant, Arthur Lowther, who himself became a partner in the early 1890s when the firm continued in the style of Smith, Brodrick and Lowther. The practice was the largest in the East Riding at that time and was responsible for many of the buildings erected in the centre of the town during the latter part of the 19th century; Savile House (348), at the corner of George Street and Savile Street, now partly demolished, is a typical example.

ARTHUR R. LOWTHER (d.1917) was an extremely versatile architect and produced many unusual buildings, all of which were quite different in design. He was closely involved with most of the buildings designed by the firm in the 1880s and 1890s.

WILLIAM SNOWBALL WALKER (d.1930) joined the partnership on Smith's death in 1901. His major commissions include Ocean Chambers, Lowgate, 1900-1; Maritime Buildings, Alfred Gelder Street, 1904; and the City Hotel, Alfred Gelder Street, 1905.

Post 1850

By 1850 Hull had been split by the railways into four distinct areas and its development may best be considered under those headings.

HESSLE ROAD AND ANLABY ROAD

In 1857 Coltman Street and Regent Street appear with very little development (VI), although a number of houses had been erected in Coltman Street as early as 1845 (40). As in Lister Street, no attempt was made to keep a uniform eaves line. In both streets the houses had gardens at both the front and back.

A change in the location of the better-class residential district was becoming clear. The Lister Street area with its walks on the Humber bank had been ruined by the coming of the railways. This led to the development of Coltman Street, Regent Street and other roads between Anlaby Road and Hessle Road as the main residential area, and by 1870 all roads to the north of Anlaby Road, except Park Street, were culs-de-sac.

1870 saw the revival of an earlier scheme to erect a promenade around the town. The Boulevard and Princes Avenue were eventually built (VIII) and there is little doubt that originally they were intended to link up. From 1870 the development of Hessle Road became noticeable, following the

PLATE XVIII – Great Thornton Street Wesleyan Chapel, 1842. Architect: H. F. Lockwood

PLATE XIX – Royal Institution, Albion Street, 1853. Architect: Cuthbert Brodrick

FRONT ELEVATION AS ALTERED BY H. F. LOCKWOOD

PLATE XX – General Infirmary

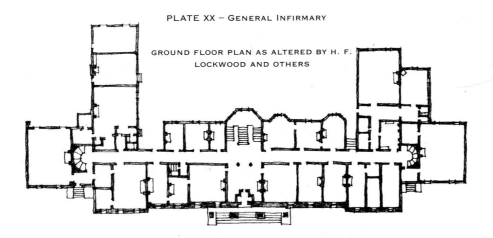

GROUND FLOOR PLAN AS ALTERED BY H. F.
LOCKWOOD AND OTHERS

construction of the docks between the Humber and the main road. This development extended as far as Brighton and Liverpool Streets by 1900 (X).

Anlaby Road was developed with very good quality buildings, the road being wide and lined with trees. Most of the houses were of three storeys and many had basements. They were nearly all faced with locally manufactured white stock bricks which were intended to imitate Portland stone. West Park was opened in 1885, a good example of contemporary park design.

Many churches, chapels and schools were erected to serve the population. In 1862 Model Dwellings (200) were built at the corner of St Luke's Street and Midland Street, for the Society for Improving the Dwellings of the Labouring Classes, to the design of the architect H. M. Eyton.

SPRING BANK, BEVERLEY ROAD AND WINCOLMLEE
Much of the land in this area was purchased by estate companies and in most cases developed as better-class housing. In 1850 land was purchased on Beverley Road by the Hull and East Riding Freehold Land Society (an organisation which enabled people to acquire the property qualification for a vote) and laid out as the Kingston Estate. It was, however, not as high quality as the Spring Street area development.

The Spring Bank Estate, started by the same Society, included Hutt, Freehold, Morpeth and Walmsley Streets (VI). The site of the Zoological Gardens was purchased by the Albion Freehold Land Society in 1863 and more elaborate development was carried out (VII). Apart from Park Street, the land on the south side of Spring Bank was not developed until about 1870. At the end of the century Derringham and Argyle Streets were connected by a bridge giving a second through road over the railway to Anlaby Road.

By 1875 the Wincolmlee district had expanded far beyond the limits of the early industrial schemes and more housing accommodation was necessary. The area between Barmston and Cottingham Drains was almost entirely built up between 1875 and 1890, and the houses were nearly all workers' dwellings. The area between Barmston Drain and the river Hull was also developed in this manner. The area bounded by Cottingham Drain and Beverley Road was in the main a better quality development and included such roads as Fountain Road and Brunswick Avenue.

In this area a large number of churches, chapels, schools and other institutions were founded. All Saints', Margaret Street, by G. E. Street, and the Seamen's and General Orphan Asylum on Spring Bank, by T. H. Wyatt, should both be mentioned.

EAST HULL
Holderness and Hedon Roads were fully established by 1850 and growth in the next 50 years was confined exclusively to their perimeter. Again, much of the development was carried out by building societies. The Southcoates Estate, crossed by Durham Street; the Victoria Estate on Hedon Road beyond Victoria Dock; and the Somerstown Estate, which includes Beeton Street, are all examples of estates laid out between 1850 and 1855. Holderness Road developed as the more popular residential area of the two, since the docks had spoiled Hedon Road for residential development. The majority of the land developed was within the area bounded by the low level ring railway line, and Sutton Drain formed a barrier between the Holderness Road area and the industrial area of the Groves.

The 1850 map shows St Mark's Street extending only as far as Sutton Drain (V), but later maps show a bridge over the drain. In 1863 the Citadel was cleared of military buildings and until 1866, when the South Bridge was constructed at the end of Humber Street, the only link across the river was by North Bridge.

Hedon Road Gaol is clearly shown on the 1875 map (VIII) and in the same year the adjoining cemetery was opened. East Park opened to the public on the day of Queen Victoria's Jubilee, 21 June 1887, and covers an area of 52 acres.

OUTSIDE THE RAILWAY RING
In 1847 the cemetery at the end of Spring Bank opened and in 1860 Zachariah Pearson, who was mayor at that time, proposed that for the first time a park should be provided in the town. He got little support, however, and therefore purchased about 37 acres of land adjoining Beverley Road. Reserving some ten acres for building purposes, he presented the central portion to the town on condition that it was laid out as a park. It was planned by James Niven, the curator of the Botanic Gardens in Linnaeus Street, and named after Pearson, in recognition of his generosity.

The fine entrance gateway (190) was manufactured by Young and Pool of Hull. It is surmounted with enrichments, shields, anchors and tridents, the arms of Hull and of Trinity House. The whole design, which is carried out in iron, forms a unique example of a Victorian triumphal arch.

In 1875 another part of the proposed promenade around the town was purchased by a wealthy young shipowner and shipbuilder named David P. Garbutt, and shortly afterwards Princes Avenue was laid out. It was in those days a handsome boulevard ornamented with trees and fountains similar to those of the Great Exhibition of 1851. As a result of the new development people soon wanted houses in the area, and speculative builders began to think of development near the park. Marlborough, Westbourne, Park and Victoria Avenues were laid out shortly afterwards and many houses were built by speculative builders between 1880 and 1910. Some of the earliest houses erected in Salisbury Street, between Park and Westbourne Avenues, were designed by George Gilbert Scott junior.

30 – General Infirmary – Main Block

32 – General Infirmary – Entrance Portico

31 – General Infirmary – Entrance Portico

33 – General Infirmary – Circular Ward

PLATE XXI – Clowes Chapel, Jarratt Street, 1851.
ARCHITECT: WILLIAM SISSONS

By 1880 the Botanic Gardens in Linnaeus Street had become too small so a new site at the southern end of Princes Avenue was laid out by Niven. The new gardens were not a financial success and the site was purchased by the Corporation in 1888 for the proposed Hymers College (opened 1893).

THE OLD TOWN

In 1855 the new high-level Hull and Barnsley Railway was opened, operating from a station in Cannon Street. This development further restricted the outward growth of the town, and by 1910 most of the area between the inner low-level railway ring and the outer ring was built up, with a considerable amount of development to the north, outside the high-level railway.

The Old Town gradually changed from a residential area into a business and office quarter. By 1860 the town had increased considerably in population and trading capacity, and many banking houses and similar institutions were erected in place of houses, particularly in Lowgate and Silver Street. The Corn Exchange (XXXIV), designed by Bellamy and Hardy of Lincoln, and built in High Street in 1856, was one of the first new public buildings to be erected in the Old Town area.

In 1865 the Exchange (115) was erected to the design of Botterill of Hull and 1869-70 a building for Hull Banking Company, at the corner of Silver Street and Lowgate (116), was designed by the same architect. Yorkshire Buildings, 1874, at the corner of Lowgate and Bishop Lane, the premises of the York City and County Banking Company and the Yorkshire Fire and Life Insurance Company, were also designed by Botterill.

WILLIAM BOTTERILL (1820-1903) started practice on his own account in 1851, working from an address in Land of Green Ginger. He was a Nonconformist and designed a number of Hull's Wesleyan chapels, including Beverley Road (XLVI), 1860, the finest of his earlier buildings. St Paul's National Schools and the Ragged and Industrial Schools (XXIX), both 1857, and now demolished, were also of high quality. Later, as architect to the School Board, he was responsible for many of Hull's early schools. His practice rapidly developed and, in addition to the Exchange in Lowgate, he designed many other important buildings. John Bilson, who was to become one of Hull's leading architects, was articled to Botterill, and later became a partner in the firm. In 1855 Botterill moved his practice to 11 Parliament Street; in 1863 he moved again to No. 23 where the firm remained until Bilson's retirement in 1930.

The effect of Nonconformist buildings on the architectural enhancement of the town was considerable throughout the years from 1830 to 1914. Even in the early period, two of Lockwood's finest designs had been for Nonconformist chapels in Great Thornton Street and Albion Street.

The siting of many of these churches and chapels, in particular those of the Wesleyan and Methodist missions, is of considerable interest. Whereas the new parish churches were invariably sited in a prominent position at the corner of two roads, the Wesleyan and Methodist churches were usually located rather differently. Most of those erected between 1860 and 1890 were sited to close the vista of a street, forming a focal point in the layout of the area. Many were situated on main roads but were usually placed opposite the junction of one of the side roads. Three of the churches designed by Joseph Wright, a local architect, are situated in this way. Lambert Street Primitive Methodist chapel (105) is another interesting example. Sited at the end of Princes Road, a continuation of Princes Avenue, it very effectively closes the vista at the end of the Princes Avenue promenade.

William Henry Kitching and Joseph Wright started in practice in the 1860s and both were to be connected mainly with the design of new Nonconformist churches.

WILLIAM HENRY KITCHING (1840-1928) set up in practice in Hull as an architect and surveyor when he was in his early twenties, with a practice in Bowlalley Lane. He later moved to 202 High Street, where he practised until the early 20th century.

He was a keen artist and between 1860 and 1870 produced a large number of pen drawings of local features, some of which may be seen in Hull Central Library. Amongst these are good, strongly coloured views of the Charterhouse and the Vicarage, Hull. In his will he left £2,000 for a stained glass window in Holy Trinity church.

One of Kitching's first buildings of importance was the Methodist Free church in Campbell Street (266), erected in 1865, but now demolished. Wycliffe Congregational chapel (XLVII) was built to his designs between 1865 and 1868, and in 1880 he designed the Unitarian church (269), in Park Street, opened in 1881. The building was demolished c.1976 and a new Unitarian church built on the site. He was also the architect for Holderness Road Presbyterian church, erected 1874-5 and demolished in 1972.

JOSEPH WRIGHT (c.1818-85), a former assistant to Cuthbert Brodrick, practised in Hull from c.1862 to 1877, from 10 Scale Lane. He designed three Primitive Methodist churches, all decidedly more French Renaissance than Italianate in character. Bright Street Primitive Methodist chapel in 1862 was soon followed by Jubilee Primitive Methodist chapel on Spring Bank (159), undoubtedly his finest work in Hull. In 1871 he designed Bourne Primitive Methodist chapel (267), Anlaby Road, in the Gothic style, no doubt influenced by Botterill's Beverley Road chapel (XLVI), but not a great success architecturally. All three chapels have now been demolished.

In 1865 Hull Seamen's and General Orphan Asylum (XLVIII) was erected to the design of T.

34 – Church Institute, Albion Street – Main Front

35 – Church Institute – Entrance hall

36 – Church Institute –
Entrance Hall

37 – Church Institute –
Ceiling to Staircase Hall

38 – Church Institute – Detail of Staircase

H. Wyatt, a well-known London architect. William Kerby, a local architect, supervised the erection of the building on Wyatt's behalf; Smith and Brodrick later added extensions in harmony with the original 1876-81.

THOMAS HENRY WYATT (1807-80) trained in the office of Philip Hardwick. In 1838 he was in partnership with David Brandon and from 1850 was helped by his son Matthew. He worked primarily as a church architect and, as a designer or restorer, was connected with more than 150 churches.

WILLIAM KERBY (fl.1862-5) was a local architect who practised from 12 Parliament Street. In 1863 he designed St Peter's Schools, Drypool, which were erected out of stone from the old citadel. He designed the extensions to Christ Church (44), 1863, and was also responsible for the designs of many of the mural monuments in St James's church. The best example of his work was the Protestant Institute in Kingston Square (119), now demolished, which was erected in 1865 and adjoined the Assembly Rooms. Later it became the Little Theatre.

The waterworks, opened at Stoneferry to the north of Hull in 1844, soon became inadequate, and in 1864 the buildings of Springhead pumping station (148), on the western boundary of the city, were erected. These were designed by Thomas Dale, described by Sheahan as the resident engineer.

THOMAS DALE is classified as an architect in the Hull Year Book for 1876, with an address at 13 Bowlalley Lane. The main building at Springhead forms an ornamental pile of red and white bricks with cut stone dressings and is one of the most beautiful industrial buildings ever erected within the boundary of Hull.

SIR GEORGE GILBERT SCOTT (1811-78) had family connections with St Mary's, Lowgate (XLV). Three generations of his family followed each other as vicar, and from 1860 to 1863 Scott was commissioned by his cousin to restore and considerably enlarge the church and design the new vicarage (264).

In 1869 All Saints' church (216), in Margaret Street, Hull, was erected to the designs of G. E. Street. His design was undoubtedly French in character and its influence on church building in the town during the next 30 years was considerable. Street also designed the vicarage (215), but the freestanding tower (212), which was linked to the church, was erected later to the designs of Samuel Musgrave, a local architect. The church, its tower and the vicarage have all now been demolished.

All Saints', built when Street's practice was very large, was not one of the finest examples of his work. It was, nevertheless, quite different from any of the earlier churches built in Hull and made a tremendous impression on the younger local architects of the time. Holy Trinity apart, it was the largest parish church ever built in the town.

GEORGE EDMUND STREET (1824-81) was one of the great church architects of the Victorian period. He intended at first to take holy orders but changed his mind and in 1844 entered the office of Scott and Moffatt. He joined the Ecclesiological Society, which had a major influence on the church architecture of the period through its journal, *The Ecclesiologist*, and in 1850 became diocesan architect of Oxford. That same year he toured France and in 1851 visited Germany and Italy.

His most famous building is probably the Law Courts in the Strand. He became an Associate of the Royal Academy and was, with Brodrick, one of the six architects selected to enter the competition for the design of the new National Gallery.

Street was connected with a large number of churches throughout the country. In addition to All Saints', Hull, he designed another eight new churches in the East Riding (including seven for Sir Tatton Sykes II) and restored or refurnished a further five. His work particularly influenced two young local architects, Samuel Musgrave and Edward Simpson.

SAMUEL MUSGRAVE (fl.1870-85), who was an Associate of the Royal Institute of British Architects, started to practise in Hull c.1870, from County Buildings in Land of Green Ginger. He later practised as an architect and surveyor from 95 Parliament Street, and in the late 1880s went into partnership with W. H. Bingley, another local man. Most of his major works were churches. It is interesting to note that he was commissioned to design the Walsham Memorial Tower to All Saints' in 1884, a few years after the death of Street. His original design was very fine (XLIII) but was unfortunately modified and reduced in height when it was built shortly afterwards.

His first church was St Silas's (XLII), erected in 1870. It was intended to be similar in arrangement to All Saints', but insufficient money was forthcoming and the fine tower over the south porch was never built. In 1874 he designed Latimer Congregational chapel (222), in Williamson Street, off Holderness Road, which was in many ways similar to St Silas's and did receive its tower. St Barnabas' (220), on Hessle Road, erected in 1873, was the finest of all his churches and was internally very similar to All Saints'. In 1877 he designed the Congregational chapel on Hessle Road (221), which externally was very fine and imposing. All of these churches have now been demolished.

In 1891 Musgrave designed Victoria Children's Hospital (224), in Park Street, in association with Bingley. The façade of this building is interesting for its massing and composition, reminiscent of the front of Street's Law Courts.

EDWARD SIMPSON (1844-1937) of Bradford, was a contemporary of Musgrave, and another church architect considerably influenced by Street. His first church was St Jude's (230), erected in 1874, which had wide aisles and small lancet windows similar to All Saints'. He also designed St Thomas's

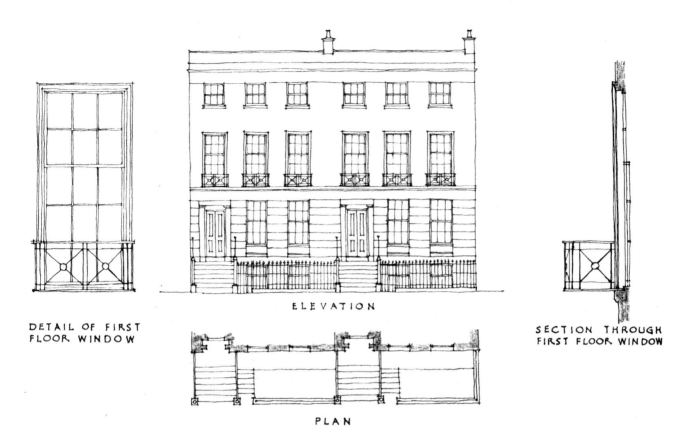

DETAIL OF FIRST
FLOOR WINDOW

ELEVATION

SECTION THROUGH
FIRST FLOOR WINDOW

PLAN

PLATE XXII – Houses at Nos. 63 and 65 Lister Street

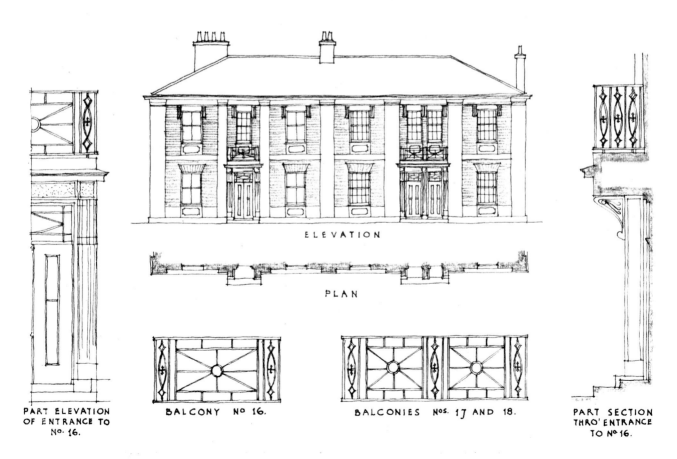

ELEVATION

PLAN

PART ELEVATION
OF ENTRANCE TO
Nº 16.

BALCONY Nº 16.

BALCONIES Nºs. 17 AND 18.

PART SECTION
THRO' ENTRANCE
TO Nº 16.

PLATE XXIII – Houses at Nos. 16, 17 and 18 St James's Square

Campbell Street (227), his most interesting church, with an apse at the east end. It was remarkable for the way in which it was planned to fit a very awkward site. None of Simpson's churches have survived.

In 1866 R. J. Withers was commissioned to design a new church in Coltman Street to serve a rapidly expanding residential area. Sheahan describes the design of the building from Withers' plans but the church, which was to have been dedicated to St Michael and All Angels, was never built.

ROBERT JEWELL WITHERS (1823-95) was a pupil of T. Hellyer, who built or restored nearly one hundred churches. Later commentators remarked that 'he built a good, cheap type of brick churches, erected with regard to style and public worship', and 'imparted to many a barn-like structure some semblance of artistic life and feeling'.

It was later decided that Coltman Street would not be the most convenient place to build a new church. An alternative site was selected on Anlaby Road, at the corner of the Boulevard, and a competition for the design of the new church, to be dedicated to St Matthew, was held. Samuel Musgrave, the Hull architect, entered the competition but was not successful. The winning design (214) was produced by Adams and Kelly, who were at that time in partnership.

JOHN KELLY (1840-1904) was head of the firm of John Kelly and Sons. He worked with G. E. Street for three years and later went into partnership with Richard L. Adams (d.1883). They practised in Leeds and worked on a number of churches in various parts of the country. In Hull, St Matthew's in 1870 was followed in 1877 by the new church of St Andrew on Holderness Road (268). This originally served a rapidly expanding residential area in East Hull but was demolished in 1984.

St John the Evangelist, a fine church erected in Prospect Street in 1866 to the designs of Alexander Gough, became St Andrew's Presbyterian church in 1868. It was badly damaged by fire bombs in the Second World War and was demolished about 1950. It is now the site of the Central Library. It was a beautiful structure in the Geometrical Gothic style. The walls were of Bradford stone (rock faced), with Steetley limestone dressings, lined internally with brick, and plastered.

ALEXANDER DICK GOUGH (1804-71) entered the office of Benjamin Wyatt and was made superintendent of the Duke of York's column. He began practice with R. L. Roumieu in 1836 and was responsible for a number of churches in the London area.

The Convent of the Sisters of Mercy, formerly on Anlaby Road, was founded in 1857; an extension designed by George Goldie was erected in 1874. It was destroyed by bombing in 1941 and demolished in 1954.

GEORGE GOLDIE (1828-1887) was inspired by Pugin and was a pupil of Matthew Hadfield. He designed a number of Roman Catholic churches, including St Wilfrid's, York, and the first Middlesbrough Cathedral.

In 1870 a competition was held by Hull Dock Company for the design of new offices to replace the old ones which by this time had become too small. The site chosen for the new building was indeed a romantic one, situated between Queen's and Prince's Docks.

The design submitted by Christopher G. Wray of London was awarded the premium, and the building (88), costing over £90,000, was erected in 1871, in the Venetian style. It is the most beautiful building erected in Hull during the Victorian era. The view of Prince's Dock, with the fine Dock Offices in the background, forms one of most widely known views of the city, and no doubt lay behind Hull's title of the 'Venice of England' in the late 19th century. Wray was also engaged to prepare a scheme for the reconstruction and redesign of the interior of St John's church, Hull.

In 1879 a scheme was proposed by James Reckitt for filling in Queen's Dock, redundant since the completion of the new docks on the east and west sides of the town. A competition was held and the winning scheme proposed to deal not only with the dock itself but also with the surrounding area, including warehouses, timber yards and sheds. A canal spanned by five bridges in the Venetian style, with tree-lined avenues on each side, would maintain water communication between the river and Prince's Dock. A large circus some 230 feet in diameter was also proposed for the centre of the area. Other buildings in the scheme included a large covered market, a public library, a swimming bath, assembly halls and a grammar school. Needless to say, the scheme was never carried out and the dock remained until 1933, when it was filled in to form Queen's Gardens.

Residential building around Pearson Park began as soon as the park itself was laid out. F. W. Hagen and William Reeves were responsible for several of the houses built at that time.

F. W. HAGEN (fl.1862-80) practised in Hull from premises at 16 Parliament Street, latterly in partnership with William Reeves. Hagen specialised in house design and was responsible for many of the very large houses erected in the new residential areas for wealthy clients, including those in Pearson Park, which have much of the appearance of Italian villas (135,136). The fine block of houses on the north side of Pearson Avenue is also his work, but the Italianate Albemarle Terrace (131), on Anlaby Road, now demolished, was his finest group of terraced houses. He was also responsible for a number of other fine houses on Anlaby Road, Spring Bank and elsewhere in the town.

In the early 1890s Thomas Spurr, a wealthy Hull solicitor, spent much of his time designing and building villas. With the aim of producing a

39 – No. 215, Anlaby Road, c.1840

40 – Houses – Coltman Street

41 – Houses – Carr Lane

42 – Houses – Beverley Road

43 – St Peter's, Drypool

44 – Christ Church – From South-West

perfectly planned house, he designed and built c.12 detached villas on the north side of Park Avenue, between Richmond Street and Salisbury Street, and 11 houses on the south side of Westbourne Avenue, west of Richmond Street. The most interesting of all his houses are the two villas on Cottingham Road (132), which he designed in the Italianate style and which were probably influenced by the earlier work of Hagen. Unfortunately, the pitched roofs to the towers on these villas have now been removed.

In 1881 John Bilson went into partnership with William Botterill, having previously been his assistant. The firm then continued as Botterill, Son and Bilson. Bilson was to follow Lockwood and Brodrick in achieving more than local fame.

JOHN BILSON (1853-1943) was born at Newark-on-Trent on 23 September 1853, and in due course came to Hull, where he was articled to William Botterill. He was admitted as an Associate of the Royal Institute of British Architects in 1881, elected a Fellow in 1911, and transferred to the retired fellowship class on his retirement from practice in 1930. He was also one of the last survivors of a generation of architect-antiquaries, including J. A. Gotch, Harold Brakespear and W. H. Knowles.

One of his earliest schemes as Botterill's partner was St Philip's, Hull, destroyed during the Second World War and demolished c.1952. This church was similar in design to many others of a slightly earlier period and, with its apsidal east end, still showed much of the influence of Street and his contemporaries. The pulpit is all that survived since it was removed to St John's, Drypool, when St Philip's was pulled down.

After Bilson became a partner, Botterill withdrew from an active role in the firm. Bilson had been with him since leaving school and had a thorough knowledge of the business. Botterill was well known in Hull as the architect of many of its Board Schools and Bilson followed in his footsteps. In 1882 he designed his first Board School in a design which he eventually perfected. He later visited Ghent and Bruges and other European cities where he studied, and was tremendously influenced by Flemish and Dutch Renaissance architecture.

In the late 1880s he introduced Dutch and Flemish details into many of his numerous Hull Board school buildings. A study of the development of the delightful *flèches* which surmount nearly all of them, is as interesting as the development of their façades and gables. He played a key role in introducing these Continental styles into the new buildings of Hull. Bilson was later influenced by the 'Streaky Bacon style' (alternate horizontal bands of brick and stone of varying widths), and at the turn of the century designed the delightful School Board Offices (354) in Albion Street.

In 1891 Hymers College was founded with money bequeathed by John Hymers, an old boy of Sedbergh School and Fellow of St John's College, Cambridge. The Botanic Gardens were purchased by the Corporation in 1888 as the site for the new college and an open competition was held shortly afterwards. Many local architects entered the competition, including Bilson and Alfred Gelder. Gelder submitted a classical design, but Bilson was placed first and awarded the premium. Hymers College shows Bilson at the height of his career. His design is usually described as a free rendering of the Jacobean style of architecture and, in its well-wooded setting, the original building is now flanked by two later additions (276). The buildings, of red brick and Ancaster stone dressings, have mellowed to form one of the most beautiful school settings in the country. On this Bilson founded a reputation which brought him similar work, including new buildings at Grantham, Rossall, Bromsgrove and Bridlington Schools. The beautiful central hall of Hymers College possesses the finest timber roof (280) of the Victorian era in the city. The main staircase (285) is also remarkable for its boldness and simplicity of detail.

Bilson's last major work in Hull was the church of St Nicholas (334), Hessle Road, demolished in 1967. It was designed as a memorial to Edward VII and was a large building with a fine tower in which a free treatment of 15th-century Gothic was used. The church opened in 1912 and showed that Bilson was by this time principally influenced by the work of Temple Moore and his contemporaries. The building was in many ways similar to St Augustine's, Hull, by Temple Moore, but easily surpassed that church in beauty.

Bilson designed many other buildings in Hull, as well as many houses in the suburbs, including a number for wealthy clients at Brough and Elloughton. He also designed many lodges for large houses in the East Riding, similar in style to the porter's lodge at Hymers College (274). A particular example is the lodge to Glenrock House at Brough.

While his merits as an architect were well recognised, Bilson also developed skills as a researcher into the history of ancient buildings and of his profession. The late Dudley Harbron, FRIBA, often told a story explaining why Bilson started to study ancient buildings and, in particular, churches.

In the early days of Bilson's architectural career, William Botterill was commissioned to carry out the restoration of Skirlaugh Church near Hull. Shortly after his appointment, a lawsuit was brought by the Vicar of Nunkeeling, on the grounds that 'a Nonconformist was not a fit and proper person to carry out restorations to a Church of England building'. The case was held at Leeds Assizes, and several prominent architects of the time gave evidence for and against. Bilson, who was present at the hearing, decided that he would never be caught unprepared and that henceforward he would devote as much time as possible to the study of Gothic architecture.

However, in fact, it is doubtful whether the lawsuit had any real bearing on Bilson's study of Gothic

45 – CHRIST CHURCH – DETAIL OF WEST TOWER

46 – CHRIST CHURCH – DETAIL OF WINDOWS

47 – ST JAMES'S CHURCH

48 – ST PAUL'S CHURCH

49 – ST MARK'S CHURCH

50 – ST STEPHEN'S CHURCH

architecture, since there is good reason to believe that he became interested in old buildings at an early age. He certainly made a measured drawing of Newark church, though he may have done this on a return visit to the town after coming to live in Hull.

From early in his career, his patience and accuracy in working out the architectural history of old buildings and reading the development of their plan had attracted the attention of older antiquaries. In 1895 he was elected a Fellow of the Society of Antiquaries, and his great knowledge and powers of exposition were often called into service by the Royal Archaeological Institute and the Archaeological Societies of Yorkshire and adjoining counties, to whose meetings and excursions he was a welcome visitor. Of a large amount of written work, he contributed much to the periodicals of these societies, especially the *Yorkshire Archaeological Journal,* which gave generous room to important monographs on Gilling Castle, St Mary's at Beverley and the Romanesque church at Newbald. His analytical account of the architecture of the Cistercians, written in the first instance with special reference to Kirkstall Abbey for the Thoresby Society, was given a more general character in the *Archaeological Journal.*

His papers entitled *The Beginnings of Gothic Architecture* not only gave a lucid account of the development of Gothic architecture, but claimed for the cathedral church of Durham a particular place in its evolution. Bilson argued that Durham was peculiarly significant among European churches as a Romanesque building already exhibiting the essential principles of Gothic art as early as the years between 1093 and 1133. His theory provoked much controversy with French scholars, jealous of the claims of the Ile-de-France. Bilson, however, remained unmoved and won the respect and admiration of his opponents, who became his firm friends. He became a leading figure at the annual meetings of the Société Française d'Archéologie, and at their meeting in Rouen in 1929 was awarded the 'Grande Médaille de Vermeil' which commemorates the founder of the Society. Many of his papers were translated into French for the *Bulletin Monumental* and other publications.

His loyalty to Durham, where he had many friends, was recognised in 1925 with the honorary degree of Doctor of Letters. Six years earlier, however, the loss of his wife had checked his vigour and buoyancy of spirit. His last archaeological paper, on the nave of Wells Cathedral, was published in the year of his retirement from active life. For another 13 years he lived at Hessle, near Hull, in the house he had occupied ever since his marriage in 1901, subject to growing infirmities of sight and memory, but never losing interest in the profession and the architectural studies in which he had achieved well deserved and, in the second case, pre-eminent distinction.

At the close of the 19th century a number of other architects were practising in Hull, who in various ways also contributed to the appearance of the town.

ROBERT CLAMP was responsible for a number of public buildings in the city. The most interesting of these is the building in Whitefriargate, formerly belonging to the Colonial and United States Mortgage Company (168). Erected in 1886, it is now the Britannia Building Society.

JOHN M. DOSSOR went into partnership with WILLIAM HENRY WELLSTED. The Strand Picture Theatre on Beverley Road (LV), demolished in 1965, was an example of their work.

THOMAS BROWNLOW THOMPSON (d.1929) was mainly connected with the design of Nonconformist churches. He built Lambert Street Primitive Methodist chapel 1893-4 (105) in association with Alfred Gelder. He designed West Hull Liberal Club c.1885 (207), now demolished, and in 1903 Boulevard Baptist church (393), demolished in the early 1970s, which was an interesting example of massing and composition.

FREEMAN, SON AND GASKELL were responsible for the design of many commercial buildings erected in Hull in the late 19th and early 20th centuries. The White Hart Hotel (369), 1904, in Alfred Gelder Street, is a fine example of their work. They also designed many of the new shops built in the centre of Hull c.1910, all easily recognisable by their terracotta facings.

WILLIAM FREEMAN (fl.1872-90) had earlier designed many Primitive Methodist chapels in Hull and the East Riding, among them Lincoln Street, 1872; St George's Road, 1873; Ebenezer, Spring Bank, 1878 (162); Hessle Road, 1880; and Selby Street, 1881. As architect to the Newington School Board, Freeman also designed a number of schools, among them Somerset Street and St George's Road (35) both 1881.

SIR WILLIAM ALFRED GELDER (1855-1941) was the last of Hull's eminent architects of the Victorian era. He was for 45 years a member of Hull City Council and five times mayor, and was knighted for his public services. He was responsible for several town planning proposals during his terms of office, and a major street has been named after him.

He started in practice in 1879 at the beginning of the great era of commercial prosperity and expansion. Energetic, forthright and tough, he was born the son of a North Cave carpenter and in his early days became friendly with Joseph Rank, who later started a flour mill on the outskirts of the town. Rank's business expanded and in 1883 Alfred Gelder designed Clarence Mills for him; in due course Rank's was to become one of the largest milling organisations in the world.

Gelder soon established one of the largest architectural practices Hull has known. His earliest work was mainly houses, and his first building in Hull was a shop in Carr Lane for Messrs William

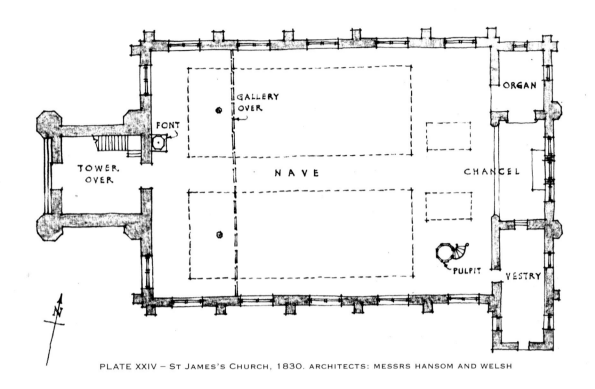

PLATE XXIV – St James's Church, 1830. architects: messrs hansom and welsh

51 – St James's Church – Interior looking East

52 – St James's Church – Interior looking West

53 – St Stephen's Church – Interior looking East

54 – St Stephen's Church – Detail of Chancel arcading

Jackson, confectioners. He was a Methodist and was to design many of the new Methodist churches in the city as well as a large number in other parts of the country.

LLEWELLYN KITCHEN (1869-1948) who served his articles with a Manchester firm of architects, joined Sir Alfred as an assistant in 1892, leaving the firm after about a year and later returning as a partner.

As Gelder and Kitchen, the firm worked on many large projects in Hull and throughout the country. Hull has been the birthplace of a number of now world-famous companies, and Gelder and Kitchen designed many new factories for them, among them Spillers, Reckitt and Colman, British Oil and Cake Mills, and Premier Oil and Cake Mills. The chief features of many of these factories are their large silos; that at Clarence Mills was particularly fine before its alteration.

Gelder and Kitchen were later responsible for many public buildings in the city, including libraries, shops, banks and offices; their own offices in Alfred Gelder Street were particularly interesting and reflected the prosperity and feeling of the times. The firm also undertook a considerable amount of work for the brewery companies, largely the responsibility of Llewellyn Kitchen.

In the early 20th century Gelder and Kitchen were responsible for many fine buildings in the Edwardian Renaissance style; the Seaton Building in Paragon Square was probably the most noteworthy.

Many of Gelder's buildings were substantially destroyed during the Second World War; the Blitz resulted, in his own words, 'in a lifetime's work gone'. Had it been 20 years earlier, he could have started again, but it was too late to do so, for a few months later he was dead.

From c.1865 clearance schemes were continually undertaken to make way for new office buildings, banks and other commercial premises, although in the main these were confined to the Old Town area. In 1880, however, Robert Jameson, Mayor of Hull, proposed an entirely new street improvement. His proposals were to extend Prospect Street and George Street through to Paragon Station, thereby enabling the demolition of the Mill Street area, which contained some of the worst housing in the city. Prospect Street was later extended to cope with the increased traffic from the new Cannon Street railway station, although the main part of the scheme did not materialise for another 21 years. Carr Lane, however, was widened in 1883, providing a better link between the Old Town and Paragon Railway Station.

In 1882, a plan showing a proposed new street between George Street and Chariot Street was drawn up by Joseph Fox Sharp, the Borough Engineer, on the same lines as Jameson's scheme. In 1893, the scheme was revived by Alfred Gelder, who proposed a similar plan. The following year a

further scheme was prepared by Hockney and Liggins, their layout following almost the same lines as Jameson's 14 years before. By 1900 a scheme for the construction of a new street from George Street to Chariot Street and the extension of Prospect Street through to the Dock Offices had received the Corporation's approval and works were already in progress.

About the same time a need was felt for a new public hall. The opportunity was therefore taken to form Queen Victoria Square in front of the Dock Offices, with the new public hall placed opposite them. The extension to Prospect Street was first called Edward VII Street and later King Edward Street. Jameson Street was named after its original author and later extended westwards to the new Paragon Square. In 1902, Gelder Avenue, now Alfred Gelder Street, was laid out together with the new Drypool Bridge to form a further approach to east Hull. Brook Street was widened to give access to Anlaby Road and, as a result, Paragon Square was formed in front of the Royal Station Hotel.

With the building of the new streets, the centre of retail trade moved to the King Edward Street – Jameson Street – George Street area, and the Old Town became increasingly concerned with commerce. The town centre had thus completed its development before the First World War. During this period many new buildings were erected, mainly in the central area, by local and by out-of-town architects.

Bacon's 1908 Plan of Hull (X) shows the city at the time of the redevelopment of the central area. It reveals that by 1908 most of the land within the Hull and Barnsley high-level railway ring had been developed; this area was to become almost entirely built up by 1914. In 1908, however, a considerable amount of development was taking place beyond the high-level railway, in the Holderness Road area, extending as far as East Park, and to the north of Hull, between Beverley Road and Newland Avenue. Pearson Park was by this time entirely developed and the Avenues were beginning to build up. The Hessle Road area was well developed, extending westwards along the whole length of the three docks. To the south of Hedon Road, in addition to Victoria Dock, the timber ponds and Alexandra Dock had been built. To the north of Drypool Bridge, the river Hull was lined with factories and their warehouses, and industry had spread up-stream as far as Stoneferry, which was now a flourishing industrial area.

The town plan of 1914 showed little change from that of 1908, development consisting largely of infilling vacant areas on the perimeter of the town.

In the early 1890s GEORGE GILBERT SCOTT junior (1839-97) was commissioned to draw up plans for the new St Augustine's church at Newland, Hull, which was to serve the now popular residential area of Pearson Park and the Avenues. Scott completed

VIEW FROM THE SOUTH-EAST.

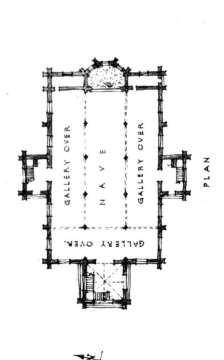

PLAN

PLATE XXV – ST MARK'S CHURCH, GROVES. ARCHITECT: H. F. LOCKWOOD

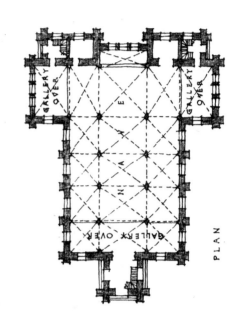

VIEW FROM THE SOUTH-WEST.

PLAN

PLATE XXVI – ST STEPHEN'S CHURCH. ARCHITECT: H. F. LOCKWOOD

the preliminary designs for the building in 1887 but Temple Moore eventually carried out the work. Scott's perspective drawings suggest that the church was intended to be in the best Scott tradition, with an abundance of pinnacles and ornament, and surmounted at its western end with an octagonal lantern.

TEMPLE LUSHINGTON MOORE (1856-1920), however, did not persist with Scott's design. He started afresh, designing the building portrayed in the illustration (322). The church, which has since been demolished, was erected 1890-6, and the porch at its western end was built in 1901. A tower over the porch (LIII) formed part of the original design, but it was never completed. This building created a sensation in Hull, like Street's All Saints' 40 years earlier, and set the pattern for future church building in the city. Bilson was greatly impressed by St Augustine's and the similarities between this church and Bilson's St Nicholas' were clear.

Temple Moore had been a pupil of George Gilbert Scott junior and worked with Scott until the latter's death. Temple Moore gradually developed his own style, designing a number of churches in Yorkshire, including St Peter's in Barnsley, St Cuthbert's in Middlesbrough, St Wilfrid's in Harrogate and St Margaret's in Leeds, as well as others at Bessingby, Carlton and Sledmere. He also restored many ancient Yorkshire churches.

By 1915 the old church of St Mary, Sculcoates, had become unsafe and Temple Moore was engaged to design a replacement, in which he incorporated many fittings, columns and other features from the old building. The new St Mary's (337) was opened in 1916 but there was insufficient money to complete the scheme. Even in its incomplete state, however, the church is very beautiful, being light and airy, especially after the rather heavy and dark churches of the mid-Victorian period.

The years from 1900 to 1914 were to see the erection of many large buildings in the city and, following R. G. Smith, the second Borough Surveyor, J. H. Hirst was appointed the first City Architect of Hull. His department was responsible for the design of a number of new buildings erected in the city at this time; these include the new Market Hall and Corn Exchange (LIV), 1902-4, which replaced the old Market Hall in Market Place; the former Police Station (355), in Alfred Gelder Street, 1902-4; City Hall (397), 1903-9; and Beverley Road Baths (363), 1905. Hirst had earlier designed Holderness Road Baths, 1897-8.

In 1900 J. S. Gibson of London built the Central Library in Albion Street (359). 1908-9 saw the building of the new General Post Office (405) in Alfred Gelder Street, designed by W. Potts of HM Office of Works. It replaced an earlier building in Market Place (86), designed in 1877 by James Williams, of the same department.

In 1903 a competition was held for the design of a Town Hall (412) to replace Brodrick's building, by then considered inadequate for the town's needs. The successful competitor was Sir Edwin Cooper. A start was made on his Guildhall in 1908 but it was not completed until 1916.

The Regional College of Art (356) was erected in 1904 to the design of Edwin Rickards and is interesting for its similarity to Deptford Town Hall, by the same architect.

In 1915 a competition was held for the design of Lee's Rest Houses (372) on Anlaby Road. The successful design was submitted by Henry T. Hare of London and is a good example of the Queen Anne style.

55 – Pulpit –
St James's
Church

56 – Pulpit –
St Paul's
Church

Comparative Roofs

57 – St James's Nave

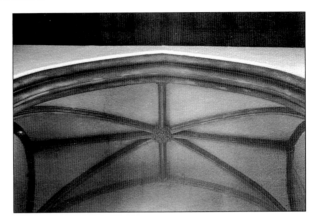

58 – St James's Chancel

59 – St Stephen's

60 – St Stephen's – Detail.

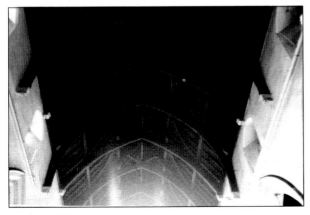

61 – St Paul's Nave

62 – St Paul's Chancel

CHAPTER III

THE EARLY PERIOD

The buildings of this period fall into two distinct groups, the early Classical Revival and the early Gothic Revival.

The Early Classical Revival

Most of the classical buildings erected during the early years were very carefully and delicately detailed, in many cases similar to the buildings of the Regency period. They also show an effective use of the orders, in some instances in the manner of the Greeks and Romans. The architecture of this period conveys an atmosphere of tranquillity, elegance and charm, very different from the pompous and sometimes vulgar appearance of some of the buildings of the later, more prosperous, periods of the Victorian era.

Given the absence of good building stone near Hull, very effective use was made of stucco, which was in many cases detailed to imitate stone. In other instances, only the classical details were executed in stucco, the remainder of the building being in brick. On some buildings the classical details were carried out in natural stone, and the remainder of the building was constructed of brickwork selected to match or contrast with the stone. Very few buildings of this period had main elevations completely of natural stone. Due to the expense of using the natural material, bricks were manufactured locally to imitate Portland and other stones. The first examples of their use are as early as 1822, in Christ Church and St Peter's, Drypool, but they were not in general use until the 1870s.

The Roman Catholic church of St Charles Borromeo (18) in Jarratt Street was opened in 1829. It was designed by John Earle junior and widened and altered, internally and externally, by Joseph J. Scoles in 1835. The narrow extensions on either side of the original building, pierced with small doors, were erected, with the adjoining presbytery, some years later, when the interior of the church was altered and remodelled in the Baroque manner.

The walls of the building, which are of brick, are extremely thick. The front, which is in the Florentine style, is stuccoed to imitate stone. The elevation as a whole is extremely bold in conception, and within the tympanum is a large shield bearing the arms, in bold relief, of the patron saint. A gallery was situated at the front end of the building, and the three windows on the front elevation were placed at the same high level as the others. These high windows enabled the whole composition to be dominated by a massive projecting portico; this while possibly a little large for the scale of the building, is undoubtedly the most carefully designed feature of the façade.

The portico, which is supported by four fluted Corinthian columns, is decidedly Roman in feeling and is flanked by two large niches. The lower portion of each niche forms a window which lights the area under the balcony. The whole design is surmounted by a massy stone cross which, whilst matching the general boldness of the whole conception, is very clumsy in design and somewhat crude when compared with the bold, but carefully designed, refinements of the building as a whole.

Since the interior has been entirely remodelled Sheahan's description of the original interior as designed by Scoles is of interest:

> 'The interior of the building is finished in the Grecian Style of Architecture. The walls are wainscoted to a considerable height, and the windows are placed very high to preserve the light in case of the ground being built up at either side. Between the windows the shield of arms of St Charles is repeated twelve times, and below them is a coloured cornice supported by pilasters in couples painted in an ornamental manner. At the street end is a gallery, on which is the organ, and the whole of the other end of the edifice is occupied as the sanctuary, the decorations of which are rich and beautiful.'

Charles Mountain junior was, as far as we know, an architect who only designed in the classical style. His buildings are noteworthy for their simplicity; he only used the Doric and Ionic orders, employed only to emphasise the main features of his designs, such as the porticoes and entrances. He was equally restrained in his use of architraves and pediments to windows, which he reserved for places of particular prominence. Friezes were usually left plain, and he only made use of triglyphs and pediments for emphasising the prominent parts of his buildings.

The Posterngate almshouses (XIII), now Carmelite House, were converted to offices 1956-7; his first buildings of importance, they were erected in 1826. In 1829-30 he designed the property on the south side of Whitefriargate adjoining the Neptune Inn. The section of the Whitefriargate building formerly occupied by the bankers Samuel Smith and Company (20) was of particularly elegant design.

This group of buildings is the only example of his work which uses brickwork as a facing material, probably because he was building up to the Neptune Inn, which was essentially of brick. Today we are only able to see the upper floors in their original form as the ground floor has been altered to form shop fronts. It is, however, one of Mountain's most pleasing and elegant designs. The four centre pilasters have delicately carved Ionic capitals and the centre five bays of the building are surmounted by a fine pediment, whose tympanum displays a finely carved group depicting the river gods and other mythological symbols. The first-floor

63 – St Mark's Church

64 – St Stephen's Church – West Doorway

65 – St Mark's – Interior Looking East

66 – St Mark's – Detail of Arcades

67 – St Paul's – Interior looking East

windows to the five centre bays of the building have stone architraves and pediments, and the second-floor windows have simply designed sills and architraves. The centre part of the building is flanked on both sides by three bays; the windows are extremely simple and without architraves in order to emphasise the main central feature of the building. The architraves, pediments and pilasters are all in natural stone, and the brickwork in Flemish bond is a pleasing red-brown colour.

The almshouses in Posterngate, although of slightly earlier date, have ground-floor window hoods similar in design to those of the Whitefriargate building. The almshouses originally had a fine central portico (XIII), surmounted by sculpture (22), but this feature was taken down in 1934, damaging the beauty of the original design, and only its base now remains (21). The portico was supported by four columns; the outer two were square and had capitals composed of a series of slight projections, a feature often used at this time. The two columns were in the Doric order, and the frieze was ornamented with eight triglyphs. The entrance and the window above have architraves, and the doorway is surmounted by a projecting head supported on brackets.

Mountain never emphasised important windows with small pediments unless the prominent parts of the building itself carried a pediment. For his Whitefriargate building he used a pediment to emphasise the central portion and therefore used small pediments above the first-floor windows of the centre block. As the Posterngate almshouses did not have a main pediment, Mountain only used flat window heads supported on brackets.

The Posterngate entrance portico is flanked by three windows on each floor; but only those on the ground floor have projecting heads supported by brackets. Each end of the building terminates with a slightly projecting bay consisting of two pilasters supporting an entablature ornamented with four triglyphs. The ground-floor windows to the end bays have projecting heads supported on brackets, and there is a slightly raised panel between the ground- and first-floor windows similar to the one over the main entrance (21). This building was the forerunner of Mountain's largest building, the Master Mariners' Almshouse in Carr Lane, which had a similar arrangement but was on a much larger scale.

The Master Mariners' Almshouse in Carr Lane (XIII) was the last building Mountain designed before retiring to Malton. Like the Posterngate almshouses they were constructed of brick and faced with stucco. This beautiful building was almost completely destroyed during the Second World War; what remained was well beyond repair and was pulled down shortly afterwards. The building had a fine projecting central portico in the Doric order (XV), flanked by wings containing eight windows to each floor. The façade was terminated

on either side by projecting pavilions of three bays, ornamented with four pilasters supporting an entablature whose frieze contained ten triglyphs.

The entrance portico was the finest part of the design, and the scheme as a whole was much more elaborate than any of Mountain's earlier designs; the drawing (XV) was made from an excellent photograph in the Wilberforce Museum, Hull. The portico consisted of four Doric columns supporting an entablature and standing on a podium. A curious feature of the columns was the way in which they were mounted on stone slabs raising them some five inches above the level of the podium. In the authentic Doric order, columns were never given bases, and in this case it seems probable that a stone base was provided to protect the bases of the columns from any standing water, which would soon have caused damage to the stucco finish forming the flutings to the columns. The columns supported an architrave and a frieze containing a total of ten triglyphs. The centre bay of the entablature contained a plaque bearing the words, 'Erected by the Corporation of Trinity House A.D.1834'. The portico was surmounted by a pediment whose tympanum displayed a fine carving of the hull of a large ship. The pilasters on the wall behind responded to the columns of the portico, while the main entrance doorway was slightly 'battered' at the sides and surrounded by an architrave. The windows in both the portico and the wings were all surrounded by architraves. The portico was approached by five steps in the centre bay with a delicate iron handrail at both sides.

The Assembly Rooms (XIII) in Kingston Square, erected 1830-4, is no longer in its original form since in 1939 it was remodelled to form a theatre (23) and has subsequently been altered again. Although the interior was completely removed, much of the original façade has been preserved. The building relies mainly on its beautiful proportions for its effect, and the detailing is very simple throughout. Here Mountain used the Ionic order and, like most of his other buildings, brick faced with stucco.

The portico facing Kingston Square and the central feature of the side elevation originally had pediments which were taken down in 1939 and replaced by parapets. The result of these alterations has been to make the building appear too heavy at the top, and it has thus lost much of its original grace and elegance. The windows were all very simply but effectively designed and only those in the main portico had architraves.

The building is 142 feet long and 79 feet broad and originally contained a vestibule 41 feet by 16 feet 6 inches. The principal room, which measured 91 feet by 41 feet and was 40 feet high, was richly decorated and could hold nearly 1,200 persons, exclusive of the orchestra which accommodated 200 performers. Adjoining was the card room and a withdrawing room. A fine staircase, 24 feet by 15 feet, led to two large rooms, formerly used as a

68 – St Paul's – South Aisle

69 – St Paul's – Detail of Nave Arcades

71 – Beverley Road House

70 – Kingston College

72 – British School, Dansom Lane

lecture room and the museum of the Literary and Philosophical Society, and later as the School and Gallery of Art. Although the building was designed and started by Mountain, it was completed under the direction of H. R. Abraham of London.

In 1832, a group of four houses known as York Terrace (XXXVIII) was erected on Beverley Road, to the designs of David Thorp. The houses are late Regency in appearance, similar in many ways to the earlier style of Charles Mountain. They are all faced with stucco, and are effectively joined together by single-storey links to form a complete group.

The end house of the terrace, at the corner of Leonard Street (174), is the most carefully detailed, having its principal entrance on Leonard Street. The front has two-storey bay windows; the centre windows are recessed, and there is a segmental pediment over the centre ground-floor window. The windows all have heavy architraves and those on the groundfloor have heavy keystones. The sills to the first-floor windows are also very heavy and are supported by brackets. The detailing as a whole is rather too much for the comparatively small elevation.

The next house, No. 79 (175), is the best of the four. The upper windows are simple and pleasing, and the wide overhanging eaves are supported by well-designed brackets. The entrance portico, supported by two Doric columns, is stumpy and ill-proportioned, and the heavy plinths flanking the steps are out of keeping with the Regency tradition. The bay windows are simple and harmless in design, although slightly on the heavy side. The iron cresting to the bays and the delicate iron balustrading above the entrance portico are the most pleasing features of the whole design. The third house (176) is again rather heavy. The entrance portico is rather better proportioned than that of No. 79, although the vases on pedestals completely spoil the effect. The original appearance of the fourth house (177) may have been quite pleasant, but the effect has been ruined completely by the addition of later ground floor bays. The links between the houses, although quite simple in design, are a little on the heavy side. York Terrace still stands, although some alterations to the elevations of individual houses have taken place.

In 1835 the monument to William Wilberforce (19) was erected to the design of John Clark of Leeds. The monument was originally placed at the end of St John's Street, but after Queen's Dock was filled in to form Queen's Gardens in 1933 it was taken down and re-erected at their eastern end. It is an elegant fluted Doric column on a square pedestal, with a statue of Wilberforce, in his senatorial robes, a folded scroll in his hand, on a small circular pedestal above the capital. The height of the base and column is 90 feet and the statue is 12 feet high. The diameter of the column is 10 feet 3 inches at the bottom and 7 feet 10 inches at the top. The entire cost of the monument was £1,250.

The School of Anatomy and Medicine (24), in Kingston Square, designed by H. R. Abraham, was an excellent example of a brick building faced in stucco to imitate stone. It has been used for various purposes since it was erected in 1833 and now only the front façade remains, incorporated into a new residential development. It is similar to much of Mountain's work, being in the Grecian style, but more elaborately detailed. The entrance portico is the most beautiful feature of the design, and the original doors remained until most of the building was demolished.

H. F. Lockwood is the only local architect connected with the buildings of this period who could be called eclectic. Although in his student days he was primarily interested in Gothic and medieval architecture, hidden talent for the classical style was shown in the early 1840s, when he designed two of the most elegant and beautiful buildings Hull has ever possessed. They were Albion Independent chapel, Albion Street, erected 1841 (XIV), and Great Thornton Street Wesleyan chapel (XVIII), of 1842, both now lost for ever. In 1907 the Great Thornton Street chapel was gutted by fire and only one of the small wings was saved. It too was eventually pulled down to make way for new flats. Albion Street chapel suffered very seriously during the Second World War; for several years its fine but badly damaged portico stood up among the ruins, reminiscent of a Greek temple.

Albion Street chapel had a massive stone hexastyle Doric portico raised on a podium 10 feet high which formed part of the basement of the building. The side and back elevations of the building were of brick to match the colour of the stone at the front, and only the windows had stone surrounds. The interior was designed in the Grecian style to match the exterior of the building. The galleries were supported by square metal pillars with Grecian caps, partly gilded. The front of the gallery and the organ were in white and gold. The ceiling was panelled and ornamented, and the building presented an appearance of massive elegance. The total cost including purchase of the site was about £8,000.

Great Thornton Street Wesleyan chapel had one of the noblest frontages in Hull; it was faced with Harehill stone and comprised a magnificent portico, whose entablature and pediment were supported by a line of eight fine fluted pillars of the Corinthian order. The entrances were in the loggia, which was supported in the centre by two circular pillars. Two wings, at some distance from the centre, were connected by open arcades or galleries, whose roofs were supported by two lines of handsome Doric pillars. The whole building was raised on a podium and the portico was approached by a very wide flight of steps. The entire frontage measured 160 feet, the portico was 66 feet wide, and the pediment rose to a height of 56 feet. The columns were 30 feet high

PLATE XXVII – TWO EARLY SCHOOLS.
ARCHITECT: H. F. LOCKWOOD

BRITISH SCHOOL, DANSOM LANE.

SCULCOATES ST MARY'S NATIONAL SCHOOL, AIR STREET

73 – SCULCOATES UNION WORKHOUSE, BEVERLEY ROAD –
FRONT BLOCK

75 – SCULCOATES UNION WORKHOUSE – GENERAL VIEW

74 – SCULCOATES UNION WORKHOUSE – INTERNAL DOOR

76 – SCULCOATES UNION WORKHOUSE – ROOF TO BOARD ROOM

and 3 feet in diameter. The side and back walls of the building were of brick, and the windows had stone sills and architraves. The photograph of the model (19a) in Wilberforce House Museum, Hull, shows rather better than the illustration the fine concept and proportions of the building.

Its interior was chastely and elegantly designed, with a fine organ enclosed in a massive case representing a Grecian temple. In addition to the chapel, the building also included a large room for tea and meetings, and nine classrooms; the chapel keeper resided in one of the wings.

Sadly, neither of these buildings remains today, for they were Lockwood's two finest works in the classical manner and showed how well he could impart scale, elegance and dignity to his designs. However, one building belonging to this stage of Lockwood's career survives and is of great importance, its design pre-dating the above by some two years. This is Trinity House chapel (26), erected 1839-43.

The chapel was Lockwood's first work as architect to Trinity House. Comparing this building with Vignola's church of San Andrea, Rome, which is very similar, both in general design and in scale (XVI, XVII), suggests that at the time Lockwood was more interested in reviving the architecture of the Italian Renaissance. Soon after he changed to the Grecian style but continued to place his buildings on an essentially Roman podium, thus making them more dignified.

Trinity House chapel is constructed of brick, and the east and west elevations are faced with stucco. The interior of the chapel is very rich and elegantly finished. The floor is paved with marble, and the pillars and pilasters are of the same material. The communion table is composed of a fine slab of highly polished marble supported by an exquisitely carved gilt eagle. The two fine pillars on either side are composed of a highly polished and valuable type of marble found only in small pieces; it is claimed that each of them is composed of 1,000 particles. The subject of the splendid stained glass east window is the Ascension of Our Lord.

In 1842 the western entrance gateway to Trinity House (27), in Prince's Dock Street, was erected. It is an interesting little building, constructed in brick and faced with stucco, and is flanked by Ionic columns. By William Foale, its design is not of the high standard of Lockwood's.

In 1840 Lockwood was engaged to carry out extensions to the General Infirmary in Prospect Street, originally designed by George Pycock. He added two new wings and applied a new façade to the front of the whole building (XX). A few years later William Botterill was engaged to design a new ward at the rear of the building, which was placed over the kitchens. Later still Saxon, Snell and Sons carried out extensive additions and alterations and added very long and rather ugly wings to each end of the existing building. To the southern wings they added a circular ward (33). At the same time, Lockwood's building was split into three parts; only the central portion (30) retained part of his façade.

The building behind Lockwood's stucco front remained much as Pycock left it, and the main staircase (7) survived untouched. The front was designed to cause as little alteration to the existing windows as possible, and the Palladian window over the main entrance in Pycock's building remain almost unaltered. The central portion of Pycock's semi-circular window on the second floor survived and, although the head of the resultant window was square, the curvature of Pycock's window could still be clearly seen (31, 32). The fine portico which was added to the main entrance was supported by four Corinthian columns. The simplicity of the ground-floor arches formed a simple but effective base to the portico over. The clock was also important, remarkable for its simplicity and effectiveness of design (31). The mechanism was housed in a small cupboard on the ground floor, on the right hand side of the main entrance, and the hands worked by a system of rods. Although the central block of the infirmary (30) was scheduled for preservation, the whole complex was demolished in the early 1970s when Hull Royal Infirmary was built on Anlaby Road, and the site is now occupied by the Prospect Centre.

The Church Institute in Albion Street (34) was originally known as Albion House and was the only example of a large private house in Hull designed by Lockwood. It was erected c.1846 for Dr James Alderson. It is a large stone edifice, which originally stood next to Albion Congregational church.

Although this building was scheduled for preservation, it fell into a very ruinous condition, and most of its fine features had been lost before renovation work commenced in 1990. The entrance and staircase hall was very fine (36), ornamented with a series of columns with carefully detailed Ionic capitals. Originally of plaster, the columns were painted during the First World War by a German prisoner of war to imitate granite, which greatly enhanced the appearance of the entrance. The doorways had nicely detailed architraves and were surmounted by fine pediments supported by corbels, on the top of which were semi-circular plaster castings (35). Two circular plaques in square frames in the entrance vestibule (36) were castings taken from the original works 'Night' and 'Morning' by Thorwaldsen in the orangery at Chatsworth House.

The treads of the staircase were of delicate design (38), and the balustrade and handrail were very beautiful, although they appeared to be of rather later date. The way in which the design of the balustrade was simplified at the turns of the staircase was very subtle indeed. The delicately coffered coved ceiling (37) over the staircase was a good example of the plasterwork of this period, although the coffered details had been rather badly

PLATE XXVIII – General Cemetery, Spring Bank – Lodge and Gate. architect: cuthbert brodrick.

PLATE XXIX – Ragged and Industrial Schools, Marlborough Terrace. architect: william botterill

handled in the corner segments. The rooflight was very beautiful and of a delicate design.

Kingston Wesleyan chapel, Witham (XIV), was another fine Nonconformist building of this period. It was erected in 1841, at a cost of £8,000, and its architect was James Simpson. The chapel suffered heavily during the Second World War, and what remained was demolished in the early 1950s. The front of the building was of stone, and the other elevations were carried out in brickwork to match the colour of the front. The projecting portico was supported by four Ionic pillars, and all the windows of the building were simply and elegantly designed with semi-circular heads.

Clowes Primitive Methodist chapel, Jarratt Street, (XXI) erected in 1851 to the designs of William Sissons, was an interesting example of the work of a local builder-architect. The entablature and pediment of the building were extremely heavy and coarsely detailed. The pilasters of the Corinthian order were simply carried out in brick, without any regard to entasis, and the only parts of the design which had been carefully detailed, with some regard to refinement, were the door and window heads and architraves. The photograph (28) shows the building in poor condition in 1955. The ugly overhanging pediment had become unsafe and had been removed a few years earlier. The chapel has since been demolished and a new building erected on the site.

In 1853 the foundation stone was laid of the Royal Institution, Albion Street, the last important building in this group. The architect was Cuthbert Brodrick, who never embraced eclecticism to the same extent as Lockwood, in whose office he had trained. Although he studied Gothic and other architectural styles, most of his buildings were in the classical manner.

The Royal Institution (XIX) covered an area of 2,200 square yards, and its principal façade was 160 feet long and 40 feet high. This building, like many others of this period, was destroyed by fire bombs during the Second World War. Its beautiful façade, though badly scarred, remained standing until about 1950 when it was pulled down to form a car park.

The building was in the Roman style, and of the Corinthian order, with the principal façade in stone. The central portion was deeply recessed to form the portico. Ten coupled columns in front were disposed after the manner of the Louvre and about 12 feet in advance of the main building supported an entablature of good proportions. The wings projected slightly and had pilasters surmounted by pediments. The whole stood upon a bold rusticated podium and was approached by two flights of steps.

The columns and entablature surmounting the portico were no doubt influenced by the Louvre as the details of both buildings are very similar. Brodrick must have studied the Louvre when he visited Paris a few years earlier, and the fact that he later went to live there for a time suggests that he was impressed by the city on his earlier visit.

Brodrick's design for Leeds Town Hall was on similar lines to Hull Royal Institution, but on a much grander scale.

A number of houses of interest were erected during this period. One of the earliest and most interesting is the fine house at No. 215 Anlaby Road (39) which was built in the 1840s, probably by George Jackson. Although essentially in the Regency style, it is remarkable for the complete absence of glazing bars to the windows. The projecting Doric entrance portico is very fine and well proportioned. The whole of the front façade is carried out in stucco, with the other elevations in brick.

The houses in Coltman Street (40) erected about 1845 are in the Mountain style but, although their entrances are carefully detailed, the houses are otherwise rather poor, with particularly weak eaves details.

The two houses at Nos. 63 and 65 Lister Street (XXII) must at one time have had quite an elegant appearance. They were pleasantly proportioned, but the weak point of their design was their badly detailed and somewhat crude entrances. These houses were of brick faced with stucco, with ground and basement floors rusticated to imitate ashlar stonework, and were demolished in the late 1950s.

The houses at Nos. 16, 17 and 18 St James's Square (XXIII) formed an interesting group; like the Lister Street houses, they were demolished in the late 1950s. These houses had stuccoed plinths and a stucco band up to the level of the ground-floor windows. A horizontal stucco band ran across at first-floor level, and the elevation was divided into bays by slightly projecting stuccoed pilasters. The panels of the design surrounding the windows were faced in brickwork in Flemish bond. The design as a whole showed a use of materials similar to that of Mountain's building in Whitefriargate (20). The detailing of the doorways and brackets to the first-floor windows was very clumsy and crude, and rather spoilt the effect of what would otherwise have been a pleasing design.

The terrace of houses erected in 1837 at the west end of the Master Mariners' Almshouse in Carr Lane (41) formed a pleasing group, but was demolished to make way for a road improvement scheme. The similarity of window heads and entrance porticoes suggests that a group of houses erected on Beverley Road about the same time, including a fine bow-windowed house (42), is probably by the same hand. Both groups of houses made use of white stock bricks for facings. A number of houses in Lister Street were also very similar. On the whole these were pleasing houses for the time, with a Georgian air about them.

Sadly, many of the important buildings of the early Classical Revival have been destroyed. Nearly all the buildings of importance of the early Gothic Revival were still standing in the 1950s but many have since been demolished.

77 – Hull and East Riding College, Park Street

78 – Ragged and Industrial Schools

79 – Borough Gaol – Entrance

80 – Borough Gaol – General View

81 – Anlaby Road Workhouse – Entrance Gateway

82 – Anlaby Road Workhouse – Lodge and Inner Gateway

83 – Anlaby Road Workhouse – Main Building

The Early Gothic Revival

The buildings of the early Gothic Revival in Hull fall into two groups: ecclesiastical buildings erected by the Church of England, and secular buildings erected for various uses. Most of the architects responsible for the buildings in this section only designed in the Gothic manner at this time; however, Lockwood stands out as the one architect who was able to design in almost any of the historic styles.

ECCLESIASTICAL BUILDINGS

The churches described here all fall into the category of Commissioners' churches, so called after the Church Building Commission, established by the Church Building Acts of the early 19th century.

In Hull the first two churches of this type were built in 1822. They were the new churches of St Peter, Drypool, (43) and Christ Church (44), near Kingston Square. Both were designed by William Hutchinson and both have now been demolished. Like St Luke's, Chelsea, they give the impression of having extremely thin walls and buttresses which were only ornamental. There is little doubt that Hutchinson was greatly influenced by St Mary's, Lowgate, since he lived in its very shadow.

The drawing shows St Mary's as it was in 1790 (XI), and it would have appeared much the same in the 1820s before George Gilbert Scott's restoration. The tower was built after the close of the Gothic period, and its buttresses look very weak and flimsy. A comparison with Hutchinson's towers at St Peter's, Drypool, and at Christ Church shows a number of obvious similarities. Both were very similar in proportion to St Mary's, and both had two horizontal stone bands, one at roof level and one still higher. The buttresses in both cases were also similar in proportion and projection to St Mary's.

The tracery of the windows in each church was the most carefully executed part of the design. Hutchinson may have been influenced by the Perpendicular windows of St Mary's or Holy Trinity, but it seems more likely that he used one of the many copy books published at that time by well-known authors to make available measured drawings and details of Gothic churches.

Undoubtedly, Christ Church was the better of the two buildings. Externally, the plans of both churches exhibited a nave, side aisles, chancel and west tower. The interior of Christ Church showed no side aisles but, excluding the chancel, comprised a large parallelogram, with galleries round three sides.

The interior of St Peter's, Drypool, had galleries on three sides supported by wooden columns formed by the union of four slender cylinders. The interior arrangement of these two churches was locally very unusual, and was more in accordance with the arrangement of a Nonconformist church.

St Peter's had an apse at the east end and was a very cheap building; it had no buttresses and was rendered to imitate stone. It was generally felt at this time that red brick was not an appropriate material for a church, and Christ Church (45, 46) was one of the earliest examples in Hull of a building faced with white stock bricks to represent stone. Its stone dressings and windows were in Roche Abbey stone.

Clarke criticises the Commissioners' churches of this period in a passage which might well have referred to Hutchinson's work:

> Perpendicular – or the transition from Decorated to Perpendicular – was generally adopted for the more ambitious buildings, and the details of many of them are reasonably accurate. . . . Architects knew enough about Gothic to bind themselves by some of its precedents, but they were not well acquainted with the style, and used it timidly and unnaturally. And they never reproduced the mediaeval proportions and arrangements.

William Hutchinson also designed the church of St John, Newland, which was consecrated in 1833. Sheahan described the building as follows:

> This edifice is a somewhat plain building of white bricks, in the shape of a parallelogram, each end raking up to an apex. The corners finish with angular buttresses, ending in conical tops. In each side are five tall lancet windows, in the west end is the entrance doorway.

Many interesting features of the building are visible in figure 318. The church was extended one bay westwards in the 1890s, and the extent of this can be seen by the coping to the parapet. Only one of the conical tops remains today, and lancets were replaced by Perpendicular windows at the time of the extensions, carried out by Smith and Brodrick in 1893. The wall bears evidence that the buttresses, which now end at the window heads, originally went higher and terminated with pointed gables, in accordance with the usual design of Early English buttresses. This can be seen clearly above the existing buttresses between the third and fourth bays from the west end.

The church of St James, in St James's Square (47), was one of the most interesting churches in Hull. It was erected in 1830 as the result of a competition won by Hansom and Welsh of York. Charles Mountain, junior, and another local architect, Williams of Blanket Row, also submitted designs. In plan and arrangement it was similar to Christ Church and St Peter's, Drypool, more like a Nonconformist than an Anglican church. It seems probable that the design specifications were largely based on the arrangement of Christ Church, and it would be interesting to know how many of the architects who entered the competition, other than

SOUTH ELEVATION OF LODGE AND ANCILLARY BUILDINGS.

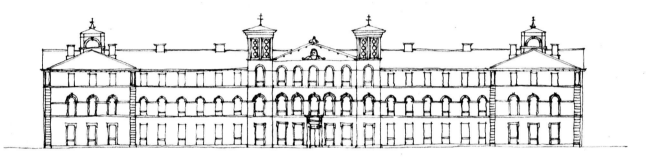

SOUTH ELEVATION OF MAIN BUILDING.

PLATE XXX – ANLABY ROAD WORKHOUSE, 1851. ARCHITECTS: MESSRS LOCKWOOD AND MAWSON

83A – TOWN HALL, MODEL

PLATE XXXI – TOWN HALL. 1862.
ARCHITECT: CUTHBERT BRODRICK

Mountain, submitted classical designs.

The winning scheme was essentially in the Early English style, although a number of classical motifs had crept in, and it was much more bold and determined than Hutchinson's designs for either Christ Church or St Peter's. St James's was built at a cost of about £6,500, of which the Church Commissioners paid two-thirds. The exterior walls of the entire building were faced with white Wallingfen stock bricks, while the plinth, dressings for doors, windows, buttresses, tower parapet and other details were of stone. The tower, which contained the entrance to the church, was 110 feet high and had large octagonal turrets at the angles.

Externally, the church exhibited side aisles, chancel and west tower, but internally it took the form of a large rectangular space, exclusive of the chancel (XXIV). The nave was illuminated by five tall windows of two lights on each side, and two similar windows at the west end, which externally appeared to light side aisles. At the east end, flanking the chancel arch, were two small circular windows of doubtful Gothic origin (51). The nave was elegantly furnished and originally had galleries round three of its sides, although by the mid-1950s only the western gallery remained (52), housing the organ console. The chancel was very small indeed and only accommodated the table and sedilia seats. The rest of the organ was placed on the northern side of the chancel, and the east end of the church was lit by three large lancets, which appeared rather distracting. During the Second World War all the windows were blown out of the building, but originally the three eastern lancets had been filled with stained glass. The centre window exhibited the Crucifixion and eight medallions contained as many subjects illustrative of the *Te Deum*.

The ceiling of the chancel was vaulted (58), the ribs gilded and the infilling painted pale blue. The chancel arch was interesting, supported by triple columns with gilded capitals. The arch itself was late Perpendicular or early Tudor in spirit, and it followed the shape of the vaulting behind.

Owing to the very short chancel, the choir faced the centre aisles at the east end of the nave. The pulpit, which was of oak (55), was beautifully carved and interestingly positioned on an open area of floor behind the choir, in the south-east corner of the nave and adjacent to the vestry (XXIV). The roof of the nave was flat and panelled in timber (57). This church was demolished in 1957.

The two churches designed by Lockwood in the early 1840s are worthy of careful study. They are St Stephen's (XXVI), erected in 1842, and St Mark's, St Mark's Street (XXV), on the east side of the river, started in 1841 and completed in 1843. Both buildings were damaged by blast during the Second World War, like many Hull churches later brought back into use; greater damage was caused subsequently by the weather, and both churches were reduced to such a bad state of repair that they were later demolished. Although both were very similar, St Stephen's was the larger and undoubtedly the finer of the two.

The designs of both buildings were influenced considerably by two local mediaeval churches, the Early English portion of Beverley Minister and Holy Trinity, Hull. It is significant that in the early 1840s Lockwood was engaged in carrying out extensive restorations to Holy Trinity, at the time that Cuthbert Brodrick was a pupil in his office and was spending much of his spare time studying and measuring local Gothic churches. This period of Lockwood's stay in Hull must have been very busy, for he was designing both classical and Gothic buildings of very high quality, and one wonders how much Cuthbert Brodrick may have contributed towards the designs of St Stephen's and St Mark's. At this time Brodrick would have had greater knowledge of Gothic architecture than of the classical styles, and it would seem impossible for Lockwood to have worked out the details of all these buildings personally.

The exterior of St Stephen's (50) was entirely of stone and was designed in the Early English style. All the churches previously discussed had their naves under one roof, and to a certain extent this was also true of St Stephen's which, although it had aisles, had no clerestory. The spire on the western tower originally attained a height of 200 feet, but in 1904 it had to be lowered to 180 feet since movement of the tower foundations had caused it to incline dangerously eastwards. The later spire appeared rather stumpy when compared with the original (50, XXVI).

A study of the exterior of St Stephen's reveals many features borrowed from the Early English transepts and choir of Beverley Minster. The spread of the buttresses and walls at the base of the building was very similar to that at the Minster. The church was cruciform in plan, and the three lancets in the east end and the gables of the north and south transepts were all obviously based on the upper lancets of the south transept gable at Beverley. The rather beautiful lozenge-shaped openings over the lancets were also a feature seen at Beverley, but rarely elsewhere. The string course which continued round the building below the lancet windows and the detailing of the buttresses were both similar to the Minster. The turrets which once graced the gables of St Stephen's resembled, but were smaller than, the fine turrets which flank the Early English gables at Beverley. The three doorways on the west, north and south sides of the tower were the most beautiful features of the exterior of the building (64). They too were similar in design to the fine Early English doorway in the south transept of Beverley Minster.

Inside, the church must once have appeared quite elegant (53). Although much smaller, the columns were almost exact copies of the piers of Holy Trinity, Hull. They had exceptionally high bases, a feature

84 –
YORKSHIRE
BANKING CO.,
WHITEFRIARGATE

85 –
YORKSHIRE
BANKING CO.
– DETAIL OF
ENTRANCE

86 – POST
OFFICE,
MARKET
PLACE

87 – UPPER
PART OF
TOWER FROM
TOWN HALL

88 – DOCK OFFICES – GENERAL VIEW

89 – DOCK OFFICES – DETAIL OF EAST ELEVATION

of the piers of Holy Trinity. The roof of the whole church was groined in a style similar to the vaulting of Beverley Minster (59). The ribs were of timber, the infilling was lath and plaster, and the whole was originally painted to represent stone. The bosses at the intersections of the ribs had once been gilded. The three lancets at the east end were originally glazed with stained glass, while all the other windows were toned down to represent old glass. The arcading below the eastern lancets in the chancel (54) was similar in design to much of the arcading in Beverley Minster.

In the early 1950s two of the piers supporting the roof collapsed, but the roof remained standing, demonstrating how well it had been framed up. Although the design appeared to be the direct result of a study of two fine local churches, their beautiful proportions were not followed. As a whole the proportions of St Stephen's were the weak point of the whole design.

St Stephen's and St Mark's were, however, the first churches in Hull during this period to be planned largely on the lines of their medieval predecessors. In both buildings an attempt was made to bring the altar nearer to the congregation by reducing the size of the chancel.

The proportions of St Mark's were much better than those of St Stephen's, and its red brick walls (63), similar in colour to those of Holy Trinity, must have appeared very pleasing. Externally the church was in the Early English style, and was constructed of red brick with stone dressings. This was the first new church in Hull to be built in red brick. Lockwood had no doubt realised the beauty of brick when carrying out restorations at Holy Trinity and subsequently used it for St Mark's.

The windows and doorways were treated very simply. In plan the church was cruciform (XXV), with a nave, side aisles, an apsidal chancel and a tower at the west end. The mouldings of the doors and windows throughout the building sprang from circular pillars, and the outer line of mouldings rested on carved human heads. The tower originally supported an elegant lantern topped by a delicate spire, but by the mid-1950s the tower carried an ugly modern octagonal brick lantern (49). The sketch of St Mark's (XXV), taken from an old lithograph, shows the church as it must have been soon after it was erected, when it stood among fields. In the background Hull Flax and Cotton Mills, on the other side of the river Hull, are visible. To the left of the church the sails of a ship on the river appear. Sheahan says of the lantern tower:

> In December, 1863, about 25 feet of the top of the spire was damaged by a strong gale of wind, and was soon afterwards rebuilt. The windows of this lantern are very fine, and the upper part of it, as well as the pinnacles in which the buttresses of the whole church finish, are in cut stone.

Internally, the piers were similar to those at St Stephen's (65), having high bases and carrying arches, giving the nave arcades a similar appearance to those at Holy Trinity, whereas at St Stephen's they were only moulded. The chancel, which terminated with an apse containing three lancets, and the tower were the only parts of the church which were vaulted. A gallery originally extended round three sides of the nave, but latterly only part of the western gallery remained. The transepts did not show in the interior aspect of the church, serving simply as entrances to the galleries, with entrance doorways in their western sides. The principal entrance to the church was provided by three doorways under the tower.

St Paul's (48), Cannon Street, is the last church to be considered in this group. It was demolished in 1976 and a new church has now been erected on the site. The first building was erected in 1847 to the designs of William Dykes, and it was then the largest church in Hull after Holy Trinity. St Paul's and St Stephen's were the only new churches to be built of stone. However, a poor building stone was chosen and the exterior of the building decayed badly.

The church was built in the Early English style, and consisted of a nave with side aisles, a chancel and, at the south-west angle of the south aisle, a belfry-tower, which was completed about seven years after the rest of the building. The tower was of an unusual design: the first stage was square, the second and third stages were octagonal, and the whole terminated with a conical roof. From the outside, the body of the church appeared rather wide and squat, but internally the nave was quite well proportioned (67) and the aisles were very wide.

This was the first new church in Hull to have a clerestory in the nave (69), which helped it to achieve a greater internal dignity than its predecessors. The pillars of the nave arcades were alternately circular and octagonal but they were not as carefully designed as those of Lockwood's churches. The nave roof (61) was very fine, springing from corbels in the clerestory, and was very similar to the timber roof of St Stephen's, Westminster, designed by Benjamin Ferrey and built about this time. The chancel roof (62) was quite pleasing in general appearance, although its eastern termination showed the awkwardness of its design. Its shape recalled the hull of a ship and it is probable that it was the work of a local shipbuilder. The carved oak pulpit (56) was an interesting example for the time. Internally this church was a copy of a typical medieval parish church, in the main quite orthodox and harmless in appearance.

SECULAR BUILDINGS

The buildings considered here are mainly schools. Again the work of Lockwood figures prominently and, with the exception of one building, is all of high quality.

90 – West Elevation

DOCK OFFICES

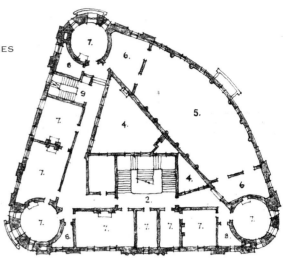

FIRST FLOOR PLAN.

91 – Lamp,
Entrance Portico

KEY TO ACCOMMODATION
1. ENTRANCE
2. STAIRCASE HALL
3. GENERAL OFFICE
4. OPEN AREA
5. STATE ROOM
6. ANTE ROOM
7. OFFICES
8. LAVATORY ACCOM.
9. STAIRCASE TO ALL FLOORS.

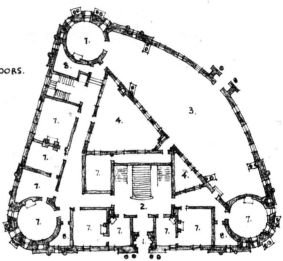

92 – West Elevation

GROUND FLOOR PLAN

PLATE XXXII – Dock Offices, 1871. Architect: Christopher G. Wray

94 – Detail of Railings

95 – Termination of East Elevation

93 –
Detail
of
Corner

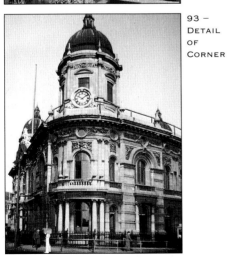

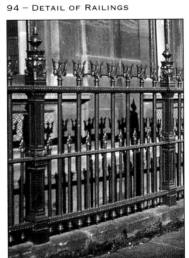

Kingston College (now Kingston Youth Centre) on Beverley Road (70), erected in 1836, was Lockwood's first major local work after coming to Hull. It was a beautiful building, essentially in the Tudor style, and of red brick with stone dressings. Almost half of the college was destroyed during the Second World War and the illustration shows the building as it appeared in 1955. The gabled portion in the foreground originally formed the centre of the composition and contained the main entrance; it was demolished in 1985. The wings on either side of the centre block were symmetrical, and the illustration shows the northern wing, which is all that now survives of the original college. The detailing of the building is good. Originally, the octagonal corner turrets of each gable were topped with stone cupolas, but owing to the damage from blast only four incomplete ones remain on the north wing; the remainder today ornament the drive leading to the front of the building. A complete cupola, which now forms one of the gateposts in front of the college, may be seen in figure 71.

Lockwood used these stone cupolas in many of his designs; in the vicarage at Kirk Ella they appear on top of buttresses. The hoodmoulds to his principal windows often terminate with a diamond-shaped motif instead of the usual carved head.

The house (71) adjoining Kingston College, probably designed by Lockwood, is an extremely interesting little building. The ground-floor windows, in the Tudor style, are in harmony with Kingston College, as is the entrance door; the details are simplified but still preserve the general effect. On the first floor Lockwood used simple windows based on Georgian proportions. The semi-classical pediments and brackets which surmount the three windows are rather badly and heavily designed and are out of keeping with the thin glazing bars and the delicate mullions of the ground-floor bay windows. The pattern used on the parapet over the bay windows of this house can also be seen on some of Lockwood's later buildings. Originally the centre window on the first floor was glazed, and the railings over the bay windows are later additions, which tend to spoil the general effect.

This is the only house not of strictly classical design whose façade was executed in stucco. This was probably done in order to bring it into line with the many late Regency style houses being erected about this time. The tops of the bays were later altered.

The British School in Dansom Lane (XXVII), erected in 1838 in the Tudor style, shows that Lockwood could design a small building equally well. The building has had many uses and has been extensively altered in the last 50 years. All that now remains are some windows and a carved angel from the base of its most beautiful feature, a very nicely designed oriel window (72). The hoodmoulds to the windows were again finished with diamond-shaped

terminations, and the pattern used on the parapet over the bays of the house adjoining Kingston College was also used over the entrance doors to this building. A small, simple stone crest surmounted the oriel window in the gable, another feature Lockwood used extensively in his designs for buildings of this nature. Altogether this was one of the most simple and most effective of Lockwood's secular buildings in this style.

Sculcoates Union Workhouse (73) on Beverley Road was also designed by Lockwood. The buildings have all been demolished and on the site stands Endeavour High School. The workhouse was erected in 1844 and was the worst design Lockwood ever carried out in Hull. Chiefly in the Tudor style, it was constructed of red brick with stone dressings. The front range was the most ornamental, and consisted of a central gateway housing a clock, the board room and, at the end, receiving wards. The central or principal range of buildings was about 220 feet long and three storeys high. Behind these were the kitchens and other offices; then came the large dining-hall, which had a pulpit at the end of it and also served as a chapel. Behind the central gateway across a courtyard was the Master's House, surmounted by an open Gothic lantern faced in stucco. To either side of the Master's House were, on the north, the male wing and courtyard and, on the south, the female wing and courtyard.

The front range of buildings (73) was very coarsely detailed when compared with Lockwood's earlier buildings. The oriel window over the gateway was clumsy, and by contrast the turrets flanking the gateway were weak. The gateway itself was reminiscent of many of the fine examples in Cambridge colleges, but was an extremely feeble interpretation. The gables to the wings on either side of the gateway would no doubt at one time have been flanked with pinnacles, but even they were clumsily and crudely detailed.

The Tudor chimney-stacks which formed the chief ornamental feature of the rear block of the building (75) were interesting but not very carefully designed. Internally, the board room was the most interesting feature, possessing a timber roof (76) typical of the period and rather spoilt by its treatment with varnish. The internal doors to the main rooms of the building were interesting (74); their design was identical to those of Kingston College.

Lockwood designed and executed all his buildings in the Tudor style long before any other local architects started to use it. By then, Lockwood had moved to Bradford and was designing in the Italianate and other eclectic fashions.

In 1846 a competition was held by Hull General Cemetery Company for the design of new gates and lodges to the cemetery in Spring Bank. In the following year, they were erected to the successful designs of Cuthbert Brodrick, who had recently started in practice on his own account. It is one of

96 – Dock Offices – Lower Part of Staircase

100 – State Room – General View

97 – Upper Part of Staircase

101 – Ceiling

98 – Staircase Hall

99 – Ceiling of Staircase Hall

102 – Detail of Orders

103 – Detail of Entrance Doors

his few designs in the Gothic style, and the lodges and gates (XXVIII) must have formed a fine group until demolished in the early 1900s to make way for shops.

The principal entrance took the form of a handsome range of six large double gates, eight stone piers and three lodges. The building shown in plate XXVIII is one of the side lodges. The scheme must have appeared very ornamental and pompous, and the detailing on this particular lodge shows Brodrick's appreciation and knowledge of Gothic architecture. Only the minor side entrance facing Spring Bank West now remains, but it has no lodge attached to it.

Sculcoates St Mary's National School (XXVII), Air Street, was erected in 1852; its architect is unknown, but it represents another design in the Tudor style. A number of other mid-century schools were designed in the Early English style. All were constructed of red brick with stone dressings but were not particularly distinguished. The earliest of these is St Mary's Roman Catholic School, Wilton Street, designed by David Aston in 1856. It was followed in 1860 by St Charles's Roman Catholic Schools, in Pryme Street. designed by R. G. Smith. Smith's last design in this manner was for the extension to St Paul's Schools as late as 1872. The most interesting, and the best, of his school designs was for Hull and East Riding College, Park Street (77), erected in 1866. The design was the result of a competition, which attracted 19 submissions.

The building, which has been demolished, had a frontage to Park Street of 131 feet. The main feature of the design, which was in 13th-century Gothic style, consisted of a hall 70 feet by 40 feet in width, accommodating 200 scholars, flanked by buttresses which, at the east end, originally carried pinnacles with carved finials. To the west of the hall were four classrooms divided by a corridor; on the south were three others of various dimensions, a lecture room, a lavatory and a cloakroom. Private rooms for masters were provided with a separate entrance from the front. The porter's residence, which terminates the front, had an entrance porch originally intended to have a lofty bell turret at one of the angles. The building was faced with red brick and dressings of Harehill stone. The whole formed an interesting composition but was by no means as fine as Lockwood 's design for Kingston College.

In 1857 the Ragged and Industrial Schools (XXIX) were designed by William Botterill. The building, now demolished, was situated on a piece of land between Cottingham Drain and Marlborough Terrace, where the entrance was situated. It was in the Tudor style, in red brick with stone dressings to doorways and windows, and it was a fine example of a carefully detailed building (78). The outer mouldings of the tops of the doors and several of the windows finished with carved heads. The staircases were of stone. The spacious schoolroom and various other apartments were lofty and well ventilated, and the building was comparable in every way with the best of Lockwood's designs in this style.

The last building in this section is the Borough Gaol and House of Correction (80) on Hedon Road, erected in 1865 to the designs of David Thorp, the Borough Surveyor, who died shortly before the foundation stone was laid. The overall design of the building is poor, and it is very coarsely detailed. Even Sheahan disliked it:

> Those portions of it that have any pretension to style are of that debased pointed character which unhappily prevailed in this country during the last century and which is generally designated Carpenter's Gothic.

The entrance (79) shows many of the same weaknesses as Lockwood's gateway to Sculcoates Union Workhouse. For its size and scale, the octagonal turrets which flank it are rather weak and crude, and the battlements at the top are totally out of scale. The mouldings of the windows and other details are equally coarse and crude, and show that Thorp did not really understand the style he was trying to imitate. R. G. Smith was appointed the next Borough Surveyor and suggested certain alterations to the design. Sheahan goes on to say:

> It is really to be deplored that certain alterations in the elevations, which were suggested by Mr R. G. Smith, architect, under whose superintendence the gaol is being erected, were rejected by the Gaol Committee.

The building, however, was quite well planned. The corridors on which the cells are situated are cruciform, and are so arranged that the governor or his deputy standing in the centre has a view of all the cells. A modern single-storey building has now been erected across the front of the gateway.

104 – THORNTON HALL,
GREAT THORNTON STREET

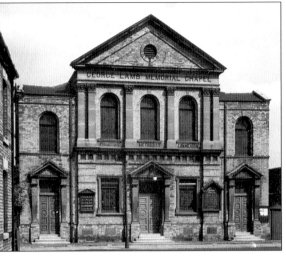

105 – LAMBERT STREET PRIMITIVE METHODIST CHAPEL

106 – THORNTON HALL –
SIDE ELEVATION

107 – BRUNSWICK WESLEYAN CHAPEL

108 – OFFICES – KINGSTON STREET, COMMERCIAL STREET

109 – PARAGON STATION – OLD BOOKING HALL

110 – PARAGON STATION – ORIGINAL ENTRANCE

111 – Royal
Station Hotel –
General View

112 – Royal
Station Hotel –
Side Entrance

113 – Royal
Station Hotel –
Paragon Square
Front

114 – Royal
Station Hotel –
Detail of
Elevation

PLATE XXXIII – Paragon Station and Hotel, 1851

Paragon Railway Station and Hotel, 1847 – south
elevation. Architect: G. T. Andrews

115 – The Exchange, Lowgate

116 – Hull Banking Co. Building.

117 – National Provincial Bank, Silver Street

118 – N. P. Bank – Detail of Entrance

119 – Protestant Institute, Kingston Square

120 – Corn Exchange, High Street

121 – General Infirmary

122 – Queen's Road Wesleyan Chapel

124 – Queen's Road Chapel – Side Elevation

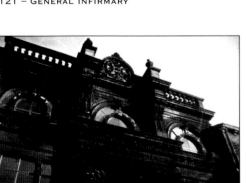

123 – Corn Exchange – Detail of Attic Floor

CHAPTER IV

THE ITALIANATE STYLE

Many buildings in Hull were considerably influenced by the Italian Renaissance, either in their details or in their general elevational treatment and massing. They can be divided roughly into six groups, although in some cases the buildings show the characteristics of more than one group.

The Venetian Influence

The earliest building to be erected in this style was the Anlaby Road Workhouse 1851, by Lockwood and Mawson (XXX). Although planned on similar lines to Lockwood's earlier Sculcoates Union Workhouse, it was in every way a superior design. Apart from some later extensions the building has now been demolished to make way for Hull Royal Infirmary. It was faced with red brickwork in Flemish bond and stone dressings. The entrance gateway (81) was a very beautiful, though simply designed, approach to the building. The adjacent railings were removed during the Second World War. The front range of buildings consisted of a fine entrance lodge (82), with double windows of a Venetian character on the first floor. The entrance porch had fine iron double entrance doors and a simple, well-designed iron fanlight over. The entrance portico was slightly projected and was surmounted by an illuminated clock. The centre block contained the board room, and the single storey wings on either side contained committee rooms and offices. The main building was of three storeys and formed a fine backing to the front range. Its most beautiful feature was the centre portion (83), which was terminated with a pediment and flanked by two Italianate towers. The upper portions of these towers contained the cistern tanks. The entrance doorway of the main building was quite simply designed and not of excessive proportions since this block was intended to be seen rising up behind the more imposing entrance gateway to the front.

In 1878 the Yorkshire Banking Company erected new premises in Whitefriargate, at the corner of Parliament Street. The new building was also designed by Lockwood and Mawson. Whilst it had certain Venetian characteristics, its effective scale is perhaps more Roman in character. Although little higher than many of the other buildings in Whitefriargate, an effect of increased elevation (84) has been achieved by substantially reducing the height of each of the upper floors in turn. The ground floor and entrance are very massive in their proportions and the rustication of the lower stonework also increases the scale. The Corinthian pilasters at the corner of the building have their entasis emphasised, and the location of the building in a narrow street helps to make it one of the most powerful designs in the whole city. The façades are effectively terminated by bold but carefully detailed cornices, and the building is altogether an exceptionally competent and beautiful design.

The old Post Office (86), in Market Place, now the Old Custom House, was erected in 1877 to the design of James Williams, and is similar in many ways to the Yorkshire Banking Company building in Whitefriargate. It is, however, inferior in design and rather unsuited to its site. The Post Office was originally framed on either side by three-storey shops which were exactly half its height. Although the front is in itself quite well designed, it appears to be stuck on to an inferior building. It is faced in Spinkwell stone.

In 1862 a Town Hall (XXXI, 83a) was erected to the designs of Cuthbert Brodrick, but it was demolished c.1912 to make way for the present, inferior Guildhall. The upper part of the tower was re-erected in Pearson Park (87), and many of the urns and vases from the top of the building now ornament gateposts at Brantingham, some 12 miles west of Hull. A mixed style War Memorial was also erected there using stone from the same source.

Brodrick's building was reminiscent of many Venetian palaces, although the tower had a more Flemish appearance. Sheahan says of it: 'the building, for architectural beauty and artistic elegance, is not surpassed, even if it is equalled, in Great Britain. Externally, it almost defies criticism'. There is no doubt that it was a beautiful building, although not as fine as Brodrick's Town Hall at Leeds. At Hull Brodrick did not have the advantage of a sloping site, and the tower was not as carefully detailed.

The building had a frontage in Lowgate of 105 feet, and the depth of the whole measured 220 feet. The main front was faced with Steetley stone and had a Bradford stone plinth and Portland stone cornices, with red Mansfield columns in front and pilasters of the same stone at the sides. The remainder of the building was faced with white stock bricks, with Steetley stone dressings and Bradford stone plinths. The windows of the main cornice were enriched with figures of naked boys holding festoons of flowers, and the parapet had an ornamental balustrade, with vases over each pedestal. At the angles of the building were four turrets, which rose about 25 feet above the cornice, and were surmounted by gilt finials. The tower, which rose from the centre of the front of the building, was 135 feet high. It was enriched with beaded mouldings forming panels. In its upper part

125 – DETAIL OF ROOF

126 – ROOF OVER SANCTUARY

127 – GENERAL VIEW

128 – SANCTUARY.

129 – WESTERN GALLERY

130 – DETAIL OF ARCADES

131 – ALBEMARLE TERRACE, ANLABY ROAD

132 – VILLAS – COTTINGHAM ROAD

was a clock with four dials, and in the tympanum above the clock were symbolic representations of Unity, Strength and Peace. The upper part of the tower was circular; it rested on eight Mansfield columns with Corinthian capitals, and had red granite panels in the spandrels of the arches and an ornamental balustrading on the upper stage, with vases on each shaft. The tower was surmounted by a large stone dome (87), highly ornamented, topped by a cast iron spear-shaped finial, double gilt, which transfixed three crowns (strictly speaking, crest-coronets), the arms of the town. The entire front was also enriched with polished granite panels, vase-shaped ornaments and other embellishments.

Sheahan describes the interior as follows:

> The principal entrance leads through a short loggia or vestibule to the grand hall and staircase, where the *coup d'oeil* is such as is seldom seen in a building in any provincial town. This hall and staircase measures 48 feet by 34 feet, and from it, on all sides, the public offices and committee rooms of the Corporation are entered. Immediately opposite the entrance is the grand staircase, which is composed of red Mansfield stone steps, Caen stone perforated balustrades, and Sicilian marble hand rails about a foot in width. This noble staircase is surmounted by an elegant arcade, formed by clustered pillars of Mansfield Stone, decorated to represent Rouge Royal, the bases Egyptian Green and Aberdeen granite. The walls of the hall are painted a subdued red, the cornice is picked in tints of red, green and buff, and the ceilings are panelled in grey with light buff styles, and decorative corners and side centres in each.

There is no doubt that the building was extremely colourful, both inside and out, but it is unlikely that it ever had the grandeur and dignity of Brodrick's generally accepted masterpiece, Leeds Town Hall.

In 1871 the new offices of Hull Dock Company (88) were erected to the designs of Christopher G. Wray. The building, also in the Venetian style, is the finest and possibly the most widely known of the Victorian buildings in Hull. The position chosen was a very good island site situated between Queen's Dock and Prince's Dock, roughly triangular in shape and bounded on its western side by Junction Street, on its eastern side by the quay of Queen's Dock, and on its northern side by Cross Street. The site boundary facing Queen's Dock was curved.

Wray's design was indeed a brave one in as much as he used the whole of the unusually shaped site. He curved his building at the corners and on each angle he placed a magnificent, circular domed lantern. The weight of these lanterns had to be carried, and this determined the circular room in each corner of the building on each floor (XXXII).

The main entrance (90, 92) is on the elevation to Junction Street and leads directly into the fine entrance and staircase hall (96, 98). At the time, Junction Street was very narrow, making it impossible to approach the building with a flight of external steps flanked by lamps. As a result, the steps were planned within the entrance porch, and a large niche containing a lamp was placed on either side (91). The lamps, which are beautifully designed, have bases similar to the candelabrum at Sant Andrea della Valle, Rome.

A fine projecting entrance portico in the centre of the curved eastern elevation gives access to a large office which dealt with business directly concerned with the docks. Above this office is situated the state room (100), which is the principal room of the building, together with an anteroom at either end (XXXII). Thus the principal room was situated in a position affording excellent views down both of the docks. Other important offices were placed on the first floor, entered directly from the staircase hall and situated over the main entrance to the building. The extent of the state room is well defined on the elevation of the building, and the anterooms are emphasised by a slight projection and a bolder treatment (95), thus forming a stop to the curved façade and a transition between it and the curved corners of the building.

The elevation to Junction Street, now Queen Victoria Square, is finer than the side facing the dock. The entrance portico, which projects slightly, consists of four Ionic columns carrying a cornice and a balcony terminated by urns (92). The first-floor window is also emphasised and flanked by two Corinthian columns; the whole is terminated by a sculptured pediment surmounted by a coat of arms. The centre portion of this façade is of five bays, and the transition between that and the curved ends of the façade is treated in a similar manner to the elevation facing the dock; the windows, instead of lighting anterooms or offices, here light the lavatory accommodation. It will be seen from the plan (XXXII) that the areas given over to lavatories are awkward spaces unsuited to any other purpose. Many of the walls of the building are as much as five or six feet thick in places.

Externally all parts of the building are beautifully detailed. It is faced almost entirely with Ancaster stone and the domes are covered with lead. The ground floor and prominent features of the design have horizontal rusticated bands at intervals. The ground-floor windows are surmounted by a coved frieze, excellently carved to imitate rope. The pilasters and columns of the ground floor are all of the Ionic order and those to the first floor are Corinthian. All the windows on the ground and first floors have semi-circular heads and the second-floor windows are all circular, although rooflights give subsidiary lighting to this floor. All the first-floor windows have ornamental balustrading below them, and these are enlarged to form balconies over the

133 – House – Pearson Park

134 – House – Pearson Park

135 – Carlton House – Pearson Park

136 – House – Pearson Park

139 – No. 7 Warehouse, Castle Street

137 – No. 7
Warehouse – West
Elevation

138 – No. 7
Warehouse – South
Elevation

140 – Railway Dock
Warehouses

141 – Hudson, Smith
and Co. Ltd.
Warehouse, King
Street

entrances and at the corners of the building. The central windows at each corner of the building are curved to follow its line, and all the windows of the lanterns are also curved. The panels above the first-floor windows are filled with beautiful and delicate carving, and in the centre of each portion is a cherub. The circular windows of the second floor are very carefully detailed, and the frieze between is ornamented with cherubs and plant forms, all excellently and delicately carved. The cornice to the top of the building is well handled and in keeping with the high standard of the building as a whole. Each of the projecting portions of the façades adjacent to the corners of the building have their cornices crowned with two well-proportioned urns.

The lanterns are all very carefully designed, in contrast to Brodrick's tower for Hull Town Hall. Each lantern has six square-headed windows with segmental pediments, alternating with columns of the Corinthian order. The whole is terminated by a well-proportioned cornice and a delicate vase surmounts each column. The lanterns are largely ornamental and each is entered from the roof, through one of the windows; the southern lantern houses a clock mechanism.

The railings which surround the whole offices (94) are very fine and embody anchors and other maritime forms in their design. Some of the original drawings, including those for the railings, may still be seen – many of them drawn freehand. However,

PLATE XXXIV – CORN EXCHANGE, HIGH STREET, 1856
ARCHITECTS: MESSRS BELLAMY AND HARDY

the majority of the drawings were given for salvage at the beginning of the Second World War.

The staircase hall (98) is a beautiful feature of the interior. The steps of the double staircase are of marble, the upper flights are cantilevered (97), and the treads are of a very delicate section. The delicate wrought-iron balustrading (96) is a supreme example of Victorian craftsmanship. The newel terminations to the base of the balustrade represent rope and acanthus forms. The doors leading to all the principal apartments are double, welldesigned, and based on Georgian proportions.

The plasterwork of the entrance and staircase hall is delicately handled and the coved ceiling is of exceptional beauty (99). The principal doorway at the head of the staircase is elegantly designed and surmounted by a fine pediment, the whole being ornamented with a leaf pattern (98). Two circular-headed archways lead from the head of the staircase to the state room and other apartments and offices. The frieze of the staircase hall is decorated at intervals with medallions containing the initials of the Hull Dock Company, and the coved part of the ceiling is decorated with a knotted diamond-shaped rope pattern. The staircase is lit by a circular rooflight in addition to three large windows over the half landing. The principal staircase terminates at the first floor, and a minor staircase on the north side of the building connects all floors.

The circular offices under the domed lanterns have, in addition to curved windows, curved doors and fireplaces. The second floor of the building was originally intended as storage space and has an interesting series of open timber kingpost roof trusses.

The Court Room (100) is the most sumptuous apartment in the building. The treatment of its unusual shape is interesting. Originally, there were no windows on its inner side (102), where the portraits of the directors of the old Dock Company used to hang. The fine columns of the Corinthian order are of composition to imitate red marble. The room continues through two floors of the building, and the ceiling and cornice (101) are very heavy, though in keeping with much of the interior work of the 1870s. The Corinthian pilasters to the doors are quite refined, in contrast with the ceiling and cornices, and are surmounted by nicely detailed cornices displaying a pattern of acanthus leaves (103). Over the cornices are two cherubs. The windows are surrounded by similar pilasters and cornices, and two cherubs effectively surround the lower portions of each circular window in the frieze. The capitals of the principal columns, the cornices and the ceiling ribs are all gilded.

The building survived almost untouched through two World Wars; it is now a listed building and has for some years been used as a maritime museum.

Lambert Street Primitive Methodist chapel (105) and Thornton Hall(104) were two very similar buildings, designed to meet similar requirements.

SOUTH ELEVATION

DOCK

QUAY.

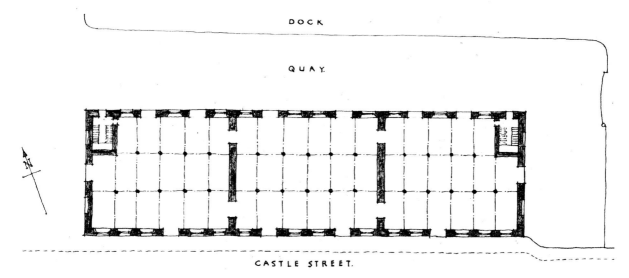

CASTLE STREET.

PLATE XXXV – No. 7 Warehouse, Castle Street, 1846. architect: J. B. Hartley

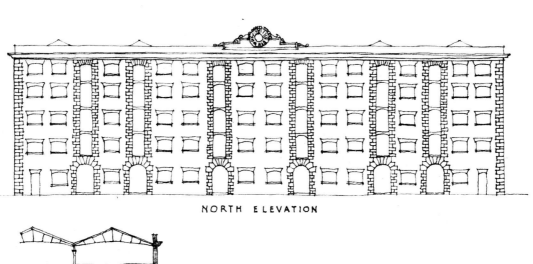

NORTH ELEVATION

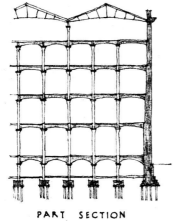

PART SECTION

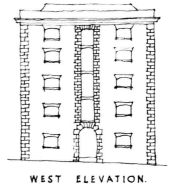

WEST ELEVATION.

PLATE XXXVI – No. 7 Warehouse, Castle Street, 1846. architect: J. B. Hartley

Lambert Street chapel was designed by Brownlow Thompson and Alfred Gelder, and erected in 1894, in white stock brick with stone dressings. Thornton Hall, opened in 1909, was designed by Alfred Gelder, in red brick with stone dressings. It was built to replace Great Thornton Street Wesleyan chapel, destroyed by fire two years earlier. Both churches have Venetian-style entrance porticoes; however, the elevation of the Lambert Street Primitive Methodist chapel is undoubtedly the more carefully handled of the two, Thornton Hall being rather heavy. The side elevation of Thornton Hall was on the whole more pleasing than the front, and its Venetian-style windows (106) gave it a pleasing appearance. Thornton Hall has now been demolished.

Brunswick Wesleyan chapel (107), Holderness Road, also now demolished, was erected in 1877, to the designs of Samuel Musgrave. Here, a more monumental approach was adopted to a programme very similar to the above: the central feature was powerfully emphasised and the central entrances were not confused with the side entrances leading to the galleries. The gallery entrances were placed on the sides of the building, forming entrance blocks which had gables and projected slightly in front of the main side elevations of the building. The columns of the front portico were of the Corinthian order, and the semi-circular brick arches were an unusual but cheap and effective feature. The first-floor windows over the doors were of a simple Venetian character. The building was constructed of white stock brick and had simple stone dressings.

The office building at the corner of Kingston Street and Commercial Street (108) shows a very simple, pleasing and effective application of the Venetian style. It is constructed of red brickwork and has only a few small details carried out in stone. The delicate eaves cornice and gutter are very effective.

The Florentine Influence

The North Eastern Railway Station (XXXIII) situated at the west end of Paragon Street, and now known as Paragon Station, was built 1846-8. The architect was G. T. Andrews of York.

Whilst the general appearance of the building is essentially Florentine, the style may be described as Doric-Ionic. The original front of the building faced Anlaby Road. The centre of the front is two storeys high (109), and is distinguished by a fine colonnade (110), beneath which were originally two entrances to the large booking office. Plate XXXIII shows the station as it originally appeared and the main entrance with its open colonnade is clearly visible. Illustrations 109 and 110 show the main block and portico after the station was greatly extended at the turn of the 19th century; the main entrance was moved to Paragon Square and the

arches of the former entrance were filled in. On either side of the main block is a one-storey wing with two good porticoed doorways (111); at the extremities of these wings are two-storey buildings.

The building is entirely faced with stone and stands on a heavy rusticated base. The columns and pilasters of the ground floor are Tuscan in character and are surmounted by a carefully detailed entablature decorated with triglyphs. Most of the pilasters between the windows are doubled. On the first floor of the entrance block the Ionic order was used for the double pilasters between the five windows. The windows have well-designed architraves and carry alternately segmental and pointed pediments (109). These buildings are 153 feet long and the original depth of the building and the platforms was 125 feet.

In 1849 the Station Hotel was erected at the eastern end of the station buildings, also to the design of Andrews. Plate XXXIII shows the hotel as it was soon after completion; it must have appeared very fine, reminiscent of many Florentine palaces with its heavy rusticated base and quoins, many circular-headed windows and low pitched roof with a heavy overhanging cornice. However, as the station grew so did the hotel, and the later top storey, together with the side wings to the Paragon Square front, completely spoiled the original effect. The original projecting stone portico of the main entrance on the Paragon Square front was later removed and replaced by a canopy (113).

The central windows to the south and east elevations on the ground and first floors have semi-circular heads, but the second-floor windows have square heads (114). The ground-floor windows are divided by columns of the Tuscan order and are surmounted by an entablature ornamented with triglyphs and carrying a balustrade to the windows above. The first-floor windows are separated by Ionic columns which support a simple entablature over which are the windows of the top storey. The second-floor windows have simple architraves and are separated by plain double pilasters which support the heavy overhanging cornice. The ground- and first-floor windows have interesting coved architraves. The corners of the building are more simply treated with heavy rusticated quoins and square-headed windows, very reminiscent of the Palazzo Pandolfini in Florence.

The double archway affording access to the station and linking the hotel and part of the station buildings on the upper floor (112) is an interesting and well-designed feature. The original station buildings and the hotel form a well-handled, simple and effectively detailed group, which is of great credit to the architect.

The Protestant Institute (119), erected in 1865, in Kingston Square, adjoining the Assembly Rooms, was a building in the Florentine style designed by William Kerby, a local architect. It has since been demolished and the site redeveloped. It was constructed of white stock bricks with cement dressings. The ground floor, which was rusticated, originally had five square-headed windows and an entrance door with a semi-circular fanlight at each end. Above the string course of the lower storey were seven mezzanine lights. The circular-headed windows of the upper floor were the most beautiful feature of the building, being separated by pilasters of the Corinthian order. The centre three bays of the building projected slightly and originally supported a well-designed pediment.

The Exchange (115), in Lowgate, now the Juvenile and Domestic Courts, was erected in 1865. It was designed by William Botterill in the Italianate style with certain Florentine characteristics. It was Botterill's first building of importance in the town centre and shows that, like Lockwood, he was an exponent of eclecticism, having earlier designed the Ragged and Industrial Schools in the Tudor style.

The building is of three storeys, exclusive of the basement, and presents an extremely bold and solid appearance. The basement and the ground floor are faced with rusticated stone, and the remainder of the building is of brickwork to match the cut stone dressings. The stone is from the Harehill quarries. The key stones of the ground-floor windows exhibit carved heads and those of the upper windows have conventional foliage. The whole design finishes with a heavy cornice. The principal entrance is in the curved corner of the building and this part of the structure is surmounted by a large figure of Britannia. The windows of the ground and second floors have segmental heads, and the first-floor windows have circular heads. The window over the main entrance is divided into three lights by Corinthian columns, and the centre portion is surmounted by a segmental pediment in addition to the cornice.

The fronts of the building are entirely devoted to offices, and on the ground floor is the Exchange Hall measuring 70 feet by 40 feet. The walls are panelled and divided by pilasters, running up to vaulted sections, meeting the springing of the arched roof. The centre forms a fine barrelled roof, with heavy coffered panels, divided by six ribs into five bays.

The building of Hull Banking Company (116), also designed by William Botterill, situated at the corner of Lowgate and Silver Street, was erected 1869-70, and is now a restaurant-bar. This building, which is entirely faced with stone, has many similarities to the Exchange, but it is more delicately handled and is in many ways more beautiful in design. The ground floor has rusticated pilasters terminating with Corinthian capitals between the windows. The corner entrance is approached by a flight of steps beneath the nicely-designed corbelled canopy, which is supported by two red polished granite columns with Corinthian capitals. The first-floor windows,

which have semi-circular heads, are divided by double pilasters of the Corinthian order. The whole is surmounted by a corbelled cornice and the building terminates with balustrading surmounted by vases. On the top of the corner balustrading are the arms of Hull Banking Company. The height of the upper storey is reduced to make the façades appear taller, and the whole stands on a heavily rusticated basement. It is a very effective and competent design which, while emphasising the stability and strength of a bank, has an air of delicacy about it.

The National Provincial Bank (117), at the corner of Silver Street and Land of Green Ginger, is a good example of the Italian palace design in vogue in the early 20th century. Erected in 1907, and designed by Dunn and Watson of London, the building is reminiscent of early Florentine palaces, although adapted to meet modern requirements. The building is entirely faced with Portland stone, and its heavy rusticated base gives it an appearance of immense strength. The projecting canopies of the first-floor windows are very bold and contrast well with the smooth ashlar facing of the upper floors. The building terminates with a deep cornice and a low pitched roof typical of many Italian palaces. The entrance is on the Silver Street front (118), and one of the chief beauties of the building is the delicate handling of the glazing bars to windows of Georgian proportions, which contrast surprisingly well with the heavy stonework.

The Roman Influence

The Corn Exchange (XXXIV), erected in High Street in 1856, and designed by Bellamy and Hardy of Lincoln, is a building essentially heavy and Roman in character. Its front is faced entirely in stone and is of two storeys, with an attic floor over, being altogether 60 feet in height. The most beautiful feature of the design is the well-proportioned entrance portico (120), which continues through two floors and is composed of two fluted three-quarter-round Corinthian columns supporting an entablature. The attic floor (123) is rather over-emphasised and tends to give the building a top-heavy appearance. The whole is terminated with a balustrade, with urns and the arms of the Corporation of Hull in the centre.

The exchange hall is 157 feet long and 36 feet in width and was spanned by 17 semi-circular laminated timber trusses supported on carved corbels, fixed in the centre of pilasters on each side of the room. The hall was badly damaged during the Second World War, and the roof trusses have been dismantled and replaced by steel trusses. The building is now used as the Hull and East Riding Museum (Archaeology).

In 1878 Queen's Road Wesleyan chapel (122) was erected to the designs of Samuel Musgrave. Although similar to Brunswick Wesleyan chapel, it was in every way a better building and displayed

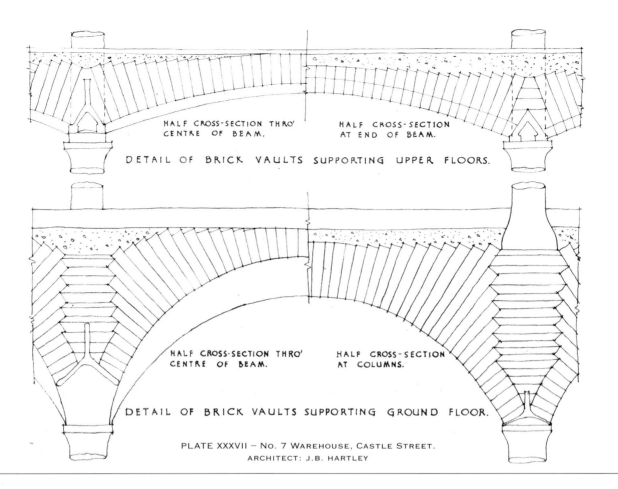

HALF CROSS-SECTION THRO' CENTRE OF BEAM.

HALF CROSS-SECTION AT END OF BEAM.

DETAIL OF BRICK VAULTS SUPPORTING UPPER FLOORS.

HALF CROSS-SECTION THRO' CENTRE OF BEAM.

HALF CROSS-SECTION AT COLUMNS.

DETAIL OF BRICK VAULTS SUPPORTING GROUND FLOOR.

PLATE XXXVII – No. 7 Warehouse, Castle Street.
ARCHITECT: J.B. HARTLEY

Wellington Street Goods Station

142 – Main Entrance

143 – East Front

144 – West Front

145 – Detail of Gables

146 – Interior View

147 – Kingpost Roof Trusses

148 – Springhead Pumping Station – General View

149 – Detail of South Elevation

150 – Pump Room

151 – South Front

152 – West Front

153 – Detail of West Elevation

154 – Detail of Beam Supports

characteristics of Roman architecture. The building was constructed of white stock bricks with stone dressings. The front was divided into five bays, the centre three containing entrances surmounted by three circular-headed windows and a pediment. The entrances were approached by a short flight of steps and were divided by four partially fluted Corinthian columns mounted on high pedestal bases. The columns supported a heavy entablature with a large projecting cornice of Roman origin, and three semi-circular arches linked the columns.

A similar treatment with pilasters and cornice was also applied to the outer bays of the front elevation and the two end bays of the side elevations. The centre six bays of the Queen's Road façade (124) were well handled. The pilasters, which continued through both floors and terminated in a series of orders of semi-circular arches, gave an excellent sense of unity to the elevation, and the more pronounced treatment of the end bays effectively terminated the composition.

As a whole this was a very pleasing and competent design, but was badly damaged during the Second World War, and was later demolished.

The small building which formed the outpatients' department of the Infirmary (121) was also of interest; now demolished, its site forms part of the Prospect Centre. It was erected in 1884 to the designs of Saxon, Snell and Sons. The main walls were of brick, and the building was faced with stone pilasters and other stone dressings. The design of the inscription and pediment over the entrance showed some similarity to the Fontana Paola at Rome, which no doubt influenced its design. The pilasters were simply detailed and of no particular order; the windows had stone architraves bearing egg-and-dart mouldings symbolising life and death.

The Baroque Influence

Hull has only one example of the Baroque style and that is the interior of St Charles Borromeo Roman Catholic church (127). The original interior was in the Grecian style; however, in 1894-6 the church was extended by Smith, Brodrick and Lowther, side aisles were added and a presbytery erected on an adjacent site. The interior of the church was then redesigned by a German, Henry Immenkamp, who carried out the work himself, finishing in 1902.

The double, fluted Ionic columns of the side arcades are of timber (130) and are decorated to imitate red marble. The double pilasters which separate the bays of the side aisles have Corinthian capitals, and the pilasters themselves are decorated with patterns carried out in delicate pastel shades. The original, small, high windows have been preserved and the space between them is filled alternately with the arms of St Charles Borromeo and paintings of biblical scenes (125). The flat ceiling of the Grecian interior has been opened in the centre to form a semi-circular bay, exquisitely detailed and carefully decorated (125). The entablature above the high altar is supported by four fluted columns of the Ionic order, and the whole is surmounted by a large representation of the Holy Trinity (128). The sanctuary is illuminated by a large, domed lantern light. The lower part of the lantern and the pendentives supporting it are beautifully embellished with scenes from the Bible (126). The gallery at the front end of the building remains substantially as it appeared in the original interior (129). The delicate cast iron columns of the original design still support the gallery, and delicate wrought iron work has been added between them. The upper part of the gallery has since been richly decorated. The whole interior is one of splendour and colour and is still in an excellent state of preservation.

The 'Italian Villa' Influence

In the 1860s and 1870s many fine houses were erected in Hull in the style of Italian villas. They were all faced with white stock bricks and had stone dressings. Most were designed by F. W. Hagen. They are nearly all detached and were designed to the requirements of specific clients.

Hagen's Albermarle Terrace (131), on Anlaby Road, was undoubtedly the finest of the terraces in this style. It consisted of five houses, each with a semi-basement, ground, first and second floor. The end house had a fine entrance doorway in the Italian style, which was approached from Gladstone Street. The other four houses had projecting porticoes supported by four columns of the composite order and approached by a flight of steps. The design of the ground-floor bay windows was very attractive. The first-floor windows had segmental arches, and the second-floor windows had semi-circular heads.

Many of the finest houses are in Pearson Park. No. 20 Pearson Park, Carlton (now Daulton) House (135), 1862-3, is the largest and most impressive, with its massive three-storey tower and low-pitched roof with large overhanging eaves. Its ground floor bay window is similar to the Albemarle Terrace bays, although much more elegantly designed. The double semi-circular windows and the predominance of brickwork over glass give it a truly Italian appearance.

The house on the other side of the park, illustrated in figure 136, is another excellent example of Hagen's work. The verandah, supported by delicate columns terminating in a pattern of ironwork, is a beautiful feature of this design.

The two beautiful houses, illustrated in figures 133 and 134, are in the Italian style but arranged more on Georgian lines. They both have very elegantly designed bay windows to the ground floor and have exceptionally massive projecting porticoes of the Corinthian order. These houses show that Hagen was an able domestic architect of his time, and his buildings adorn many of the main roads and residential areas of Hull.

Towards the end of the 19th century, Thomas Spurr, a local solicitor, designed and built a number of houses in the Avenues, mainly in the classical style. However, he also designed two houses on Cottingham Road, illustrated in figure 132, which have certain Italian characteristics but are not of the same standard as Hagen's work. Their tower roofs are now flat.

The Italian Influence on Industrial Buildings

The earliest industrial building in Hull showing Italian influence was the very fine No. 7 Warehouse in Castle Street (139), designed in 1844 by J. B. Hartley and erected in 1846. The building formed one of the finest ranges of Victorian warehouses in the whole country; although scheduled for preservation, it was demolished in 1971.

The building was constructed of brickwork with very thick walls and had heavy rusticated stone quoins to the corners, the loading bays and the entrances (137,138). With its comparatively small grilled windows and large expanse of brickwork beneath a very heavy cornice, the building resembled an early Florentine palace. It was of five storeys built over a basement. The height of each floor was successively diminished, thus making the building appear taller when seen from narrow Castle Street. The centres of the north and south elevations, which were different, were surmounted by large clocks (XXXV, XXXVI). The end elevations had blank windows (137) in order to produce a uniform effect round the whole building.

The construction of the floors was interesting and consisted of a series of brick barrel vaults supported on circular cast iron columns and beams (XXXVII). The top of the vaulting was in each case levelled with concrete and the floors were finished with paving. The upper floors, which did not carry so much load, had comparatively flat arches, but the ground floor, which bore the largest load, was carried on almost semi-circular brick vaults. Owing to the considerable weight of the building on the poor subsoil between the two docks, the warehouse was built on timber piles (XXXVI). The roof trusses were of very delicate steel construction by comparison with the solidity of the rest of the building. The walls diminished in thickness towards the top.

However, problems were caused by the weight of the stone cornice and clock, and the absence of any effective ties: by the mid-1950s the centre of the top floor wall on the south elevation was overhanging the base of the building by 14 inches. The warehouse as a whole was extremely fine and was an outstanding attempt to provide a functional building of artistic beauty, but had to be demolished due to its instability.

The Railway Dock warehouses (140) were built to meet similar requirements, but they were designed on purely functional lines and lacked the same architectural beauty. The upper floors of these warehouses were all of timber and noteworthy for single balks which spanned some 60 feet to carry the floors. The building displayed some fine, mellowed red brickwork and with its seven storeys was one the tallest Victorian structures in Hull. Its small windows in a vast expanse of brickwork gave it quite an overpowering appearance when seen from the narrow Kingston Street. Only one end of this building now remains.

The warehouse of Hudson, Smith and Co. Ltd. in King Street (141), is a noteworthy example of early Victorian work, and its beautiful mellowed red brickwork and pedimented ground-floor windows give it a very elegant appearance for an industrial building.

In 1858, following the construction of Railway Dock, the old passenger station in Kingston Street was pulled down. On its site a fine goods station (142) was erected to serve the new dock. The building was in the Italianate style, of red brick with stone dressings. The east elevation (143), facing Humber Dock, consisted of the entrances with offices over. Its cornice was surmounted by a series of 12 pediments of varying size. The west elevation, giving access to the trains (144), consisted of a similar series of pediments and a fine series of arched openings carried out in brickwork, one to each railway line.

The most interesting feature of the building was the roof construction. Each bay of the building, which carried a pediment at each end, was divided by a fine series of cast iron Tuscan columns, between which ran girders supported on moulded iron brackets (146). The space between the girders was spanned by a fine series of timber roof trusses (147), which formed the most interesting feature of the whole scheme. Although this building was listed for preservation, it was eventually demolished.

Springhead Pumping Station (later the Yorkshire Water Museum) (148) was erected in 1862-4 to the designs of Thomas Dale. The tall building adjacent to the chimney was the portion erected in 1864 and houses the massive Cornish beam engine which can still be seen today. Shortly afterwards, the smaller building with the square tower and fine octagonal cupola was erected to house additional smaller pumps.

Thomas Dale must have been a very able man, both as an engineer and an architect. Sheahan says of him:

> With the exception of the two bores made by Mr Warden, the whole of the Springhead works, including the buildings, were designed by, and carried out under the superintendence of Mr Dale – no other engineer or architect being employed.

The buildings, which are in the Italian style, form a very fine group, both in massing and composition, and the whole is undoubtedly the finest industrial building in Hull.

The buildings are faced in red and white brickwork with stone dressings, all of which have now mellowed beautifully, giving them the charm of many Georgian designs. The original building, which is of three storeys (151), is divided into five bays, each separated by a slightly projecting pilaster (153). The windows of all floors to each bay are grouped within a tall semi-circular headed arch of two orders. The inner order is of white bricks, while the arch of the outer order is emphasised with dark red bricks, and the whole is ornamented with a stone keystone. This treatment is similar to the side elevation of Queen's Road Wesleyan church (124). The ground-floor windows are very tall, rising from the plinth of the building. The second-floor windows consist of a pair of small semi-circular headed windows with stone sills. The arches of the first- and second-floor windows are picked out in darker bricks. The walls are completed with a well-proportioned stone cornice supported on well-designed brackets.

The main entrance to the building is between a pair of pilasters on the gabled south side. The cornice to the side elevations is returned over the pilasters only, and the pilaster effect is carried round the reveals of the gable. The entrance door, clerestory window and first-floor window above are grouped within a tall semi-circular arch of two orders (152), similar to the side elevations, with the inner order formed of white bricks. The entrance itself has a semi-circular head and a large keystone, and the clerestory window over is circular. The second floor comprises a group of three circular-headed windows, the centre one being slightly taller; all three have keystones and sills and are surrounded by a 4½ inch wide projecting brick architrave.

The later building is two storeys in height and is also of five bays (152), the end elevations having low pitched gables. The centre bay of the south elevation is emphasised by a projecting tower, surmounted by a pediment, octagonal lantern and cupola of Italian style. The bays of the south elevation are again divided by pilasters (149), and the ground- and first-floor windows are grouped within a tall semi-circular headed arch of two orders. The inner order is again composed of white bricks. The ground-floor windows are tall and rise from the plinth of the building and have large keystones. A continuous horizontal stone course of greater dimensions than that of the original building forms the sills to the first-floor windows, and the walls again finish with a well-proportioned stone cornice supported on well-designed brackets. The cornice and brackets continue round the tower, whose south elevation incorporates a stone pediment. The south elevation of the tower has a tall semi-circular headed window of two orders on the ground floor and on the first floor a circular window ornamented with four keystones. The entrance to this building is on the east side; the doorway is similar to that of the original building and is surmounted by a circular window.

The two buildings are connected by a short link corridor designed to harmonise with the scheme as a whole. The chimney (since demolished) was octagonal in plan. It was constructed of brick with stone dressings and capping, and was of excellent proportions, perfectly in harmony with the rest of the design.

The pump room of the original building is very fine (150). The massive beam of the engine is supported by four fluted Tuscan columns surmounted by three elegant arches and a deep cornice (154). This feature, together with two smaller columns supporting part of the mechanism, lend an atmosphere of grace and dignity to an otherwise functional aspect. The whole concept, both inside and out, is very fine and a great credit to one of Hull's few engineer-architects.

Several brewery buildings erected in this period also have an Italian feel about them. Malting No. 4 (156), Anlaby Road, was built in 1862, probably to the design of William Simmons, for Gleadow, Dibb and Co., the forerunner of Hull Brewery. It had a particularly good elevation for an industrial building. The small windows, contrasting with the greater expanse of brickwork, and the heavily emphasised quoins were reminiscent of No. 7 Warehouse in Castle Street. The front had a nicely detailed cornice surmounted by a pediment, which was solid and in keeping with the rest of the design. The tympanum was pierced with a semi-circular window of Venetian origin. The building gave an appearance of great strength and was an example of good industrial design for its time. It was demolished some years ago.

The Jarratt Street elevation of the the Gleadow, Dibb brewery in Silvester Street, now The Maltings, was designed 1867-9 by William Sissons (155). It is very pleasing and effectively closes the south side of Kingston Square. The general height of the building is three storeys but the centre portion of six bays is five storeys high. The double windows of the ground floor have semi-circular heads and the windows of the upper floors have shallow segmental arches. The upper floor of the centre block is extensively glazed, and this portion is surmounted with a pleasing octagonal lantern with a copper cupola. The cast iron bridge spanning Silvester Street (158) is a very beautiful feature; it bears an anchor, the trade mark of the company, and is supported by two delicate iron brackets at each end.

Moor and Robson's Crown Brewery (157), in Raywell Street, was an interesting building; the cornice and window details of the upper floors were similar to Springhead Pumping Station, although the whole design was of a much heavier character. This building was demolished in 1964.

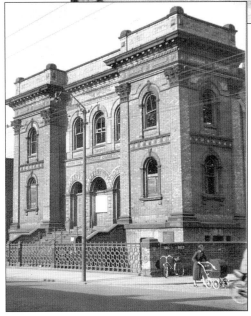

CHAPTER V
THE FRENCH RENAISSANCE INFLUENCE

The French Renaissance style of architecture also influenced a number of buildings in Hull. Initially the French influence was not very strong and it did not become popular until the 1860s; the Italian influence, however, can be detected in buildings erected some 20 years earlier.

The first building to be constructed in the French style was Bright Street Primitive Methodist chapel (161) in 1862, designed by Joseph Wright, a local architect. The following year, Wright also designed Jubilee Primitive Methodist chapel (159) on Spring Bank, which was more strongly French in character and much the finer and more interesting of the two. These buildings were about the same size and had many other similarities; however, both were demolished in the late 1950s. Both buildings were carefully sited, Bright Street chapel opposite Field Street, and Jubilee chapel opposite Park Street, the once important road linking Anlaby Road and Spring Bank. Both chapels were constructed of red and white bricks with stone dressings, and both had interesting features in fine iron railings and entrance gates which were designed to slide apart. A wide and imposing flight of steps led up to triple entrance doors in each case.

Jubilee chapel (160) had a very bold and powerful appearance, standing out as the most prominent building on Spring Bank. The entrance doorways were flanked by coupled pillars of stone with carved capitals. A wing at either side advanced five feet in front of the vestibule, thereby forming a deep recess to the main entrance. The wings were carried above the general elevation and crowned with mansard roofs, surmounted with ornamental cresting and finials, which gave the building a somewhat French appearance. Since these wings also projected five feet beyond the sides of the building they assumed the appearance of towers. A bold cornice, which extended across the whole of the front, carried a parapet, and the centre finished with a pediment ornamented with carved stonework.

In contrast with the rather bold exterior, the interior (163, 164) was very refined and elegant for the period. It was galleried, with an apsidal recess at the opposite end of the gallery to the principal entrance, in which the organ was placed. The gallery front was of enriched panels picked out in delicate pastel shades. Slender cast iron columns with Corinthian capitals supported the gallery (164). The ceiling was ornamented with a large central rose (167), originally with a gasolier of about 50 lights, and later with an electric light. The central rose was of a very delicate design and was one of the most elegant examples of Victorian plasterwork in Hull. This feature was picked out in pastel shades. The angles of the ceiling were coved and had

enriched bands with an elegant cornice below. Another beautiful feature of the interior was the raised pulpit (165), supported by two fluted cast iron columns with Corinthian capitals. A winding staircase (166) approached the pulpit platform. The staircase and pulpit had very attractive iron balustrading with a polished mahogany handrail, and the whole displayed a refined elegance rarely found in later 19th-century architecture.

In 1877 William Freeman designed another chapel in this style. This was Ebenezer Primitive Methodist chapel (162), also situated on Spring Bank. It was rather smaller than the above, and since it was not raised up on a basement, it was less impressive. This building ceased to be a church in 1944 and, after being used as a warehouse for a number of years, it was demolished in 1976. It was constructed of red and white bricks with stone dressings. Generally speaking the building was more on the lines of the Bright Street chapel, although the towers with steep mansard roofs and ornamental cresting and finials had a particularly French appearance.

The Colonial and United States Mortgage Company building, now the Britannia Building Society (168), shows more French influence than any other in Hull. Erected towards the end of the 19th century to the design of Robert Clamp and Alfred Gelder, it is situated at the corner of Whitefriargate and Land of Green Ginger. The fine original corner entrance has been replaced, and only one of the original ground-floor windows still remains on the Land of Green Ginger elevation; this window is similar to those on the upper floors but larger. The heavy stone mullions and transoms and the elaborate dormer windows are reminiscent of many French chateaux. The mansard roof, together with the chimneys and ornamental cresting, are all designed in character with the rest of the building. The detailing is very good, and the design as a whole is the most exciting of all Clamp's buildings, which are usually dull and uninteresting.

The warehouse of Hull Ships' Stores Company (170), now flats, stands next to the site of the old North Bridge. The building is the most interesting of the many warehouses which line the banks of the River Hull but is in no way as fine as the former No. 7 Warehouse in Castle Street. Its chief features of interest are the fine mansard roofs surmounted by finials. The detailing of the cornice is quite pleasing and the dormer windows are simply and attractively handled. The chimney stacks are interesting, although they show perhaps more Tudor than French Renaissance influence.

The shop building at the corner of Midland Street and Anlaby Road (169) is typical of the many buildings in Hull which try to be French in character. Its badly formed mansard roof, its cresting and finials, its chimney stacks with heavy cornices and its crude dormers lend a French appearance, but as a whole it is very poor and uninteresting. The building no longer has its chimney stacks.

A number of houses built about the same time as the Italian villa type showed the influence of the French Renaissance. The Linnaeus Street house, illustrated in figure 171 and now demolished, was probably the most outstanding example, with its tall tower terminating with a mansard roof, surmounted with cresting and finials. The first-floor window of the tower had an interesting canopy of French feeling. The centre dormer window to the main block of the house was also French in character, but the side dormers were probably later editions.

Rockliffe House on Beverley Road (172), built 1864, and now Hull and East Riding Institute for the Blind, displays the solidity of many French Renaissance chateaux. Built of white stock bricks, it has heavy stone dressings and details. The plan is obviously that of a symmetrical building at the front, but an unsuccessful attempt has been made to treat the elevation as an asymmetrical composition by adding a gable and bay window to the left side of the elevation. The entrance is emphasised by a tower with a mansard roof, surmounted by cresting and finials.

Tamworth Lodge (173) on Beverley Road (now the Dorchester Hotel) incorporates Dorchester House, built 1861-2 by Bellamy & Hardy. It has towers terminating in spires covered with ornamental slates and decorated with tiny dormers. The large windows are divided into separate panels with thick transoms and mullions.

All these houses are constructed of white bricks and have stone dressings.

163 – Jubilee Chapel Interior – General View of Gallery

164 – General View

165 – Pulpit

166 – Staircase to Pulpit

167 – Detail of Ceiling

168 – Colonial and US Mortgage Co. Building

169 – Shop – Anlaby Road

170 – Hull Ships' Stores Co. Ltd. Warehouse – North Bridge

CHAPTER VI
THE MID-VICTORIAN STYLES

Some of the more interesting mid-Victorian buildings cannot be linked with a particular historical style. The buildings vary considerably in their design, and some of those built during the late 1860s and 1870s tend to be rather debased and pompous, due perhaps to the increased prosperity of the times and the consequent over-elaboration of buildings.

West Parade House (178), off Anlaby Road, was erected in the 1840s and was similar to the earlier York Terrace. It was constructed of brick and rendered to imitate stone. Its bow windows had little of the charm of their Georgian equivalents, and the building as a whole gave the appearance of having sunk several feet into the ground. The entrance portico, supported by two stunted Corinthian columns, was very badly proportioned, and its Corinthian-like capitals tended to be rather flamboyant and somewhat vulgar in their appearance. The portico was surmounted by a Palladian-styled window which was very heavy and Victorian in character, lacking the elegance of earlier windows of this type by Pycock, for example at the Neptune Inn (8). The chimney stacks were in a style typical of the period, and the general appearance of the whole building was one of ugliness. The house, which has now been demolished, was the home of Alfred Gelder for a number of years.

In 1846 the Royal Queen's Theatre (179) was erected in Paragon Street. The theatre accommodated over 3,000 people and, at the time, was one of the largest in the country. Its façades were of brick with a stuccoed finish. The principal front in Paragon Street was 200 feet in length, and the second front in South Street was 70 feet long.

Towards the end of the 1860s, the theatre caught fire and the interior was destroyed. The building by this time was proving too large and about half of it was sold. This part was later pulled down and the Imperial Hotel erected on its site. The western end adjoining South Street was remodelled internally into a smaller theatre and opened in 1871 as the Theatre Royal, later to become the Tivoli.

The original elevation to Paragon Street was a massive frieze supported by nine pilasters, with very large windows between them. The front of the smaller theatre building was part of the original façade. The cornice and pediment were very coarsely detailed. The pilasters of the parapet wall above the cornice were also very heavy, and the architraves to the windows were clumsy. Although the side elevation was rather more pleasing than the front, it could not be compared with the Assembly Rooms (XIII), a similar but earlier building. The theatre has now been demolished and the site redeveloped for shops and offices.

The house in Leicester Street (180) is a typical example of a house of the late 1840s. The architraves to the windows were very heavy, and the entrance portico and steps were rather coarsely handled. In contrast with the general appearance of solidity, the large overhanging eaves of delicate Regency design appeared rather weak. John Somerscales, the artist, 1847-1946, once lived here. This house, with many original details removed, still survives.

The fine double-fronted house on Anlaby Road (XL), erected about 1850, is an excellent example of a typical Victorian villa. It stood very near to the elegant No. 215 (39), on which its proportions were probably based. It was constructed of white stock bricks with stone dressings. The entrance was very simple but very effective; the pedestalled vases flanking the steps were quite in place here and enhanced the design. The ground-floor bays were elegant, and the artistic wrought iron cresting contrasted well with the simplicity of the bays. The architraves to the first-floor windows were well proportioned, and a single stone band formed the window sills. The roof was of a low pitch and had very narrow eaves. The weakest elements of the whole design were the two small side doors which tended to weaken the extremities of the building. This villa has now been demolished.

The Public Baths and Wash-houses (201), erected in Trippett Street, to the designs of David Thorp, the Borough Surveyor, were interesting. The building, which was opened in 1850, was constructed of red and white brickwork with stone dressings. The design was unusual, similar in feel to much of the English Renaissance work of Sir John Vanburgh. The cornices were carefully detailed and as a whole the building was of higher standard than Thorp's design for the Borough Gaol. It was demolished some years ago.

The building at the corner of Wincolmlee and Charlotte Street (202), with its flat overhanging stone cornice, had a rather Continental appearance. The pronounced stone architraves to the closely placed upper windows gave the building an appearance unique in Hull. The ground floor suggested that it may once have been quite elegant, with large windows divided by Ionic columns. If this was indeed the original design, the upper floors must have appeared rather heavy. This building has now been demolished.

About 1856 the Revd H. R. Kemp built a house in Park Street (184). Originally used as a private school and extended in 1869 by William Botterill, with further additions in the 1870s, it became the Sailors' Orphanage and in 1898 opened as Hull Municipal Technical College. The building is constructed of white stock bricks with cut stone

171 – House – Linnaeus Street

172 – Rockliffe House, Beverley Road

173 – Tamworth Lodge, Beverley Road

174 – York Terrace, Beverley Road – No. 77

175 – York Terrace, Beverley Road – No. 79

176 – York Terrace, Beverley Road – No. 81

177 – York Terrace, Beverley Road – No. 83

E A S T   E L E V A T I O N.

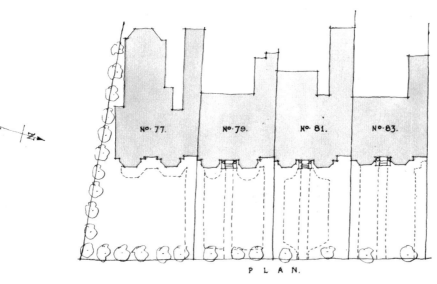

NO. 77.   NO. 79.   NO. 81.   NO. 83.

SCALE OF FEET FOR ELEVATION:
10 5 0   10   20

SCALE OF FEET FOR PLAN:
10 5 0   10   20   30

P L A N.

PLATE XXXVIII – YORK TERRACE, BEVERLEY ROAD

178 –
WEST
PARADE
HOUSE,
ANLABY
ROAD

179 –
ROYAL
QUEEN'S
THEATRE,
PARAGON
STREET

180 – HOUSE –
LEICESTER STREET

181 – MUNICIPAL
TECHNICAL COLLEGE,
PARK STREET –
ENTRANCE

182 – Houses – Beverley Road

183 – Station Hotel, Mill Street

184 – Municipal Technical College, Park Street

185 – House – Pearson Park

186 – House – Beverley Road

187 – House – Beverley Road

188 – Lansdowne House, Anlaby Road

189 – Houses – Beverley Road

dressings. It is a typical example of the dull mid-Victorian classical style, and its most beautiful feature is the fine sculptured pediment. The entrance portico (181) is of stone supported by four columns of the Tuscan order, and the whole is very severe. The building is now used as an annexe of Hull College.

In 1860 Pearson Park was laid out. The fine entrance gateway in cast iron (XXXIX) was erected in 1863. Even today, without its gates, it forms a very elegant entrance to the park (190). The design, by Young and Pool of Hull, was probably inspired by Robert Adam's western gateway to Syon House, which is very similar in style but is constructed in stone. The Pearson Park gateway is a very fine example of Victorian craftsmanship in cast iron. The fine statues of Queen Victoria (191) and Prince Albert, placed in the park in 1863 and 1868 respectively, were the work of Thomas Earle, the locally born sculptor.

The small drinking fountain of 1864 (192) in Pearson Park is another delicate and pleasing example of iron work. In the 1870s cast iron fountains (193) were also erected in Princes Avenue and the adjacent avenues. All were based on the designs of the fountains at the 1851 Exhibition.

In 1862 Model Dwellings (now Turner Court) was erected at the corner of St Luke's Street and Midland Street, to the designs of H. M. Eyton (200). This scheme represents one of the earliest attempts to improve the living conditions of the working classes by erecting flats or tenements. The street elevations of the buildings are faced with white stock bricks and red brick bands. The interior elevations of the buildings, which border three sides of a courtyard, are faced entirely with white stock bricks (203). The ground-floor flats are entered directly from the streets and also have doors opening onto the courtyard (XLI).

The elevations facing St Luke's Street and Midland Street are mainly of two storeys; the centre portions only are three storeys in height. The flats on the upper floors are approached from open galleries overlooking the courtyard. The galleries to the western three-storey block are supported by slender iron columns, and those to the remainder of the flats are supported by timber posts with bracing, giving them something of a medieval appearance. The railings to the balconies are of simple and delicate design. An interesting lamp (203), raised on a brick pedestal, stands in the centre of the courtyard. The scheme as a whole is interesting for its time and is quite well designed.

In the 1870s and 1880s slender barley sugar columns were used to decorate bay windows and other features. The Station Hotel (183), adjacent to Mill Street, was an excellent example of this style. The ornamental pilasters with Corinthian capitals were very beautiful, and the thin barley sugar columns with Ionic capitals were very elegantly designed. The ground-floor cornice was punctuated with ornamental carved brackets of great beauty. The segmental arches to the first-floor windows had carved keystones depicting the heads of men and women. Each of the upper windows was ornamented with a delicate wrought iron motif, and the façade terminated with an ornamental eaves cornice. The building, which as a whole was very pleasing and truly Victorian in character, has now been demolished.

A number of houses erected about this time also have barley sugar window details. The double-fronted house on Beverley Road, illustrated in figure 187, is the best example; the bay windows have quite an elegant effect owing to the use of these columns.

The Kingston Hotel (209), designed by William Marshall of Wright Street, in 1877, and situated at the corner of Trinity House Lane and North Church Side, is the most interesting of a number of brick buildings in the old town which are finished in stucco and have a very Victorian feeling. The hotel, which is extensively glazed on the ground floor, with rusticated pilasters between the windows, is a very pleasing design. The first-floor windows have square heads and are surmounted by a delicate cornice, supported by brackets in the form of men's heads. The second-floor windows have semi-circular heads, and the areas between the window heads are moulded and ornamented with circular medallions bearing three crest-coronets, the arms of the city. The frieze above the second-floor windows comprises a pattern of circular medallions which is very effective and is surmounted by a well-designed cornice. The cornice is effectively terminated at each end with a corbelled lion's head, which is supported by the end pilasters of the building. The façade is completed by a balustrade with pilasters.

In 1874 one of the first Board Schools to the design of William Botterill, architect to the Hull School Board, was erected in Lincoln Street (210). Its design, carried out in red brick and stone, was very interesting, and unique in Hull. The small tower over the southern gable, which effectively gave the building much of its character, had a predominantly Anglo-Saxon feeling with its small paired windows and corner columns. Many of the ground- and first-floor double windows were divided by a column of Anglo-Saxon style. As a whole it was a much more interesting building than many of the later Board Schools, and the windows were quite large and airy. It was demolished in 1997.

In the late 1870s a number of fine large houses were erected in the popular residential areas of the town. The two-storey house on Beverley Road, illustrated in figure 186, forms a continuation to York Terrace and has the same eaves line in order to harmonise. Before the addition of the shop window it must have been a very pleasing building. Corinthian capitals were used for most houses of this type as a decorative feature of the corner mullions of the bay windows. The entrance portico

PLATE XXXIX – ENTRANCE TO PEARSON PARK BEFORE REMOVAL OF GATES IN 1939.
ARCHITECTS: MESSRS YOUNG AND POOL

191 – PEARSON PARK – STATUE OF QUEEN VICTORIA

193 – FOUNTAIN – WESTBOURNE AVENUE

190 – PEARSON PARK – ENTRANCE GATEWAY

192 – PEARSON PARK – DRINKING FOUNTAIN

PLATE XL – VILLA, ANLABY ROAD, CIRCA 1850

194 – HOUSES – PRINCES AVENUE

197 – OLD FIRE STATION, HALL STREET

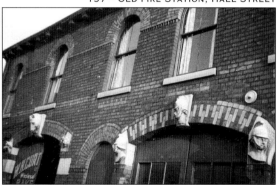

195 – HOUSES – PARK AVENUE

198 – NEWINGTON PRESBYTERIAN CHURCH, ANLABY ROAD

196 – SHOPS – BEVERLEY ROAD

199 – WESTERN LIBRARY, BOULEVARD

is very fine and well proportioned, and the first-floor window is well designed. The corner mullions to the bay windows have a delicate carved line pattern, and the heavy cornices to the ground- and first-floor bays, supported by rich brackets, are typical of the prosperity of the period.

The fine pair of three-storey, semi-detached houses on Beverley Road, illustrated in figure 182, whilst perhaps not as carefully detailed as the last example, are nevertheless very imposing. The fine projecting timber entrance portico is a feature largely peculiar to houses of this period in Hull, and the double portico of these two houses is a fine example. The individual entrances are of good proportion, and the pediment over the cornice effectively holds the design together. The carved work above the pediment is perhaps a little large but nevertheless helps the design. The pediment has been removed.

The house in Pearson Park, illustrated in figure 185, is a straightforward composition largely based on the Georgian type of house. The first-floor windows are comparatively simple, and the more ornamental features are all on the ground floor. Only the centre attic window is original; those at the sides have been added later. The entrance portico, although carefully detailed, is very wide, and as a result the bay windows and entrance tend to appear crowded. Generally speaking the house is quite pleasing and similar in many ways to some of the nearby Italianate villas.

A little later houses became heavier and more pompous in design; Lansdowne House, on Anlaby Road (188), with its heavy rusticated quoins, was a typical example. The Corinthian capitals to the portico and ground-floor bays again show a tendency towards flamboyance and vulgarity. This house has now been demolished.

The block of houses between De Grey Street and Lambert Street (189) shows this development taken a stage further. The houses are very heavy and pompous. The first-floor windows with their heavy pediments are badly proportioned and with their ugly brackets have a rather vulgar, debased appearance.

Towards the end of the 1870s, a number of rather dull and heavy buildings were erected; the Gas Offices (204), built in Baker Street in 1879, are typical. They were designed by Robert Clamp and are very uninspiring, displaying a rather debased form of the classical style. Hull Savings Bank, in George Street (205), now demolished, was another example of Clamp's work and almost as dull. The projecting porticoes were rather clumsy and heavy in design, and very poor in comparison with that of Botterill's Hull Banking Company building (116), at the corner of Lowgate and Silver Street.

West Hull Liberal Club, in the Boulevard (207), designed c.1885 by Brownlow Thompson, was slightly more interesting. The projecting entrance portico was quite fine, although the columns did not follow any of the standard Greek or Roman orders. The iron balconies to the first floor were quite pleasing, but on the whole this was still a heavy and drab design; the building has now been demolished.

The Gas Offices (206) in St Mark's Street, erected in 1884, were another example of the uninspiring buildings of the period. They were constructed of hard stock bricks with stone dressings and have now been demolished.

The old Fire Station (197), in Hall Street, off Spring Bank, whilst generally of little architectural importance, is interesting for the carved heads above the two entrances. The entrance to the stables is ornamented with three stone replicas of horses' heads. The entrance for the engine itself is surmounted with three stone replicas of firemen's heads, complete with helmets.

The houses on Princes Avenue overlooking Pearson Park, (194), are an interesting example of the better class of speculative builder's work of the 1870s. Whilst the light stone dressings contrast well with the now pleasingly mellowed red brickwork, the designs as a whole are very clumsy and heavy on close examination.

The houses in Park Avenue, built in the late 1880s, and known as Salisbury Gardens (195), are much more competent in design, and form one of the finest groups of houses in this area after those designed by George Gilbert Scott junior in Salisbury Street. The houses are faced with white stock bricks and have red brick heads to windows and doors. Although these houses are very small inside, they appear comparatively large from the outside.

The shops on Beverley Road, (196), are typical of many of the blocks of smaller shops on the main roads leading into the City. The towered corners bring some excitement to what would otherwise have been a rather monotonous group.

The shop on Holderness Road (208) is a typical example of a more formal approach to shop design. The building was originally two shops and has been converted into one. The detailing as a whole is quite delicate and pleasing, and a good example of what could often be a dull style of architecture.

PLATE XLI – MODEL DWELLINGS, ST LUKE'S STREET,
1862. ARCHITECT: H. M. EYTON

SCALE OF FEET:
10 5 0 10

KEY TO ACCOMMODATION
1. ENTRANCE.
2. LIVING ROOM.
3. SCULLERY.
4. BEDROOMS.

PLAN OF ONE DWELLING.

SCALE OF FEET:
0 50 100

BLOCK PLAN

MIDLAND ST.

ST. LUKE'S ST.

200 – MODEL DWELLINGS

201 – PUBLIC BATHS – TRIPPETT STREET

202 – SHOP – WINCOLMLEE, CHARLOTTE STREET

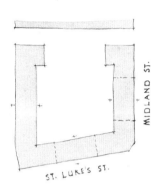

203 –
MODEL
DWELLINGS –
COURTYARD

204 – GAS
OFFICES,
BAKER
STREET

205 – HULL
SAVINGS
BANK,
GEORGE
STREET

CHAPTER VII

THE GOTHIC REVIVAL

The buildings of the Gothic Revival are discussed here in three sections. The first deals mainly with those new churches erected in Hull between 1860 and 1890 under the influence of G. E. Street and his fellow Ecclesiologists. It includes a study of All Saints', Hull, designed by Street, and examines its influence on local architects of the period. The second considers School Board Gothic, essentially an extension of the style used by Street and his followers. The final section discusses the restoration of St Mary's, Lowgate, by Sir George Gilbert Scott, and a number of other churches in the Geometrical Gothic style.

G. E. Street and his Influence on Local Architects

From 1866 to 1869 Street was engaged on the new church of All Saints' (216), Margaret Street. The famous All Saints' in London, by William Butterfield, was situated in a street of the same name. Street was churchwarden there, but his Hull church was much simpler in character and showed only a few similarities to Butterfield's work. The church, which cost over £9,000 and seated over 1,100 people, was built of red stock bricks with stone dressings. It was essentially the first church of the Ecclesiologist type to be erected in Hull; since it was designed by a well-known architect of the time, it formed the prototype for nearly all the parish churches built in the town during the next 25 years. It was also the first church in Hull to have an interior faced with red bricks instead of being plastered.

Street usually preferred a church with narrow side aisles, considering wide aisles a hindrance to worship. He believed that the arcade should be kept as an architectural feature, but that the aisles could be reduced to the width of passages, and the nave made broader. All Saints' had a very wide nave, but here Street also used exceptionally wide aisles containing no seating and making the church very broad overall.

The church was in the Early English style but essentially French in plan. The chancel was under the same roof as the nave and terminated with an apse (213). An ambulatory was planned round the outside of the apse, but through shortage of money was used to form the vestries. As a result the lower arcading in the chancel was solid and ornamented with religious scenes carried out in mosaic. The chancel was illuminated entirely by six large clerestory windows (213), those to the aisles being the smaller (216).

The nave, however, was back lit by three large lancets in the gable at the west end; thus the

sanctuary, with its large clerestory lighting, could not fail to be the focal point of the whole interior. The wide side aisles of the nave continued round the west end; a link was later provided from this aisle to an otherwise free-standing tower at the south-west corner of the church. Street was already dead by the time the money for the tower became available, so Samuel Musgrave, a local architect, was engaged to carry out the design.

The nave was composed of five bays, and the octagonal piers had simple bases and moulded capitals. The stone of the piers continued round the undersides of the wide pointed arches, which were further emphasised by moulded brick architraves. The brick architraves rose from stone pendants over the capitals of the piers. These pendants were decorated with a delicate geometrical plant pattern. Between the arches of the arcades were large, circular decorative features which had various delicate mosaic patterns in colour and moulded brick surrounds, probably inspired by a similar feature at All Saints', London. The clerestory windows of the nave were linked with simple but effective decorative arcading, the heads formed in a stone band and above a moulding from which sprang the brick pointed arches. Although the nave and chancel were under the same roof, the chancel was narrower, allowing the nave walls to be higher and the clerestory larger than would otherwise have been possible.

The roof of the nave (241) was open and of a simple timber construction. Circular iron beams tied the bases of alternate roof trusses together, and the intermediate trusses were tied by iron rods. The chancel roof was plastered and strengthened by thin horizontal tie rods (246). A tall pointed arch separated the nave from the chancel and, within this arch, a lower arch sprang from the same capitals. The space between the two arches was filled with open geometrical tracery reminiscent of the famous girder arches at Wells Cathedral. This double open arch was one of the most beautiful features of All Saints'.

There was an open arcade of three bays on each side of the chancel, of a simple design in harmony with the nave arcades. Over the arcade on the north side was a clerestory arcade of six bays divided by slender double cylindrical shafts with bases and capitals (218), and behind these were the organ pipes and mechanism. The centre bay of the arcade on the south side was surmounted by a clerestory window of the same design as that of the apse.

The stone font, situated in the centre bay of the western aisle was very simple in design. The pulpit (251) was also of stone and of a simple and pleasing design. Many later churches of this type in Hull

206 – Gas Offices, St Mark's Street

207 – West Hull Liberal Club, Boulevard

208 – Shop – Holderness Road

209 – Kingston Hotel, Trinity House Lane

210 – Lincoln Street Board School

211 – Palace Theatre, Anlaby Road

212 – All Saints – View from the East

213 – All Saints' – Detail of Apse

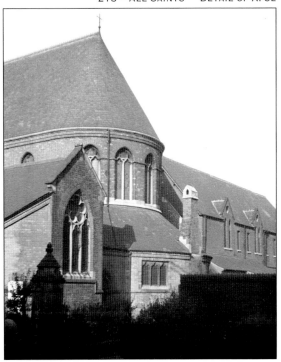

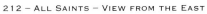

also have very simple stone fonts and pulpits, probably inspired by those at All Saints'. The attractively carved choir stalls contrasted well with the simple pulpit (218).

Externally, the side walls appeared low beneath the large, steeply pitched roofs (212, 216). The details of the eaves were very simple and consisted of a series of slightly corbelled brick courses. The north and south aisle windows were in the form of simple lancets, and the centre bay of the western aisle was emphasised by a gable containing a large window ornamented with geometrical tracery. There was an entrance porch in the western elevation of the corner aisle bays, and the single bay link with the tower was ornamented on its western elevation with a blank arch similar in size to an adjoining doorway (216).

The west gable of the church was the most ornamental feature of the whole exterior. The gable was pierced by three tall lancets, of three lights in the central lancet and two lights at the sides (216). A stone band ran across the elevation at eaves level. The gable was completed by a stone coping and there was a pattern of blank lancets over the main window. Either side of the windows were two blank lancets.

The clerestory windows of the nave were detailed identically on the exterior and the interior, each linked by a series of three blind arcades. The heads of the arcades were formed in a stone band which was returned round the west gable.

The apsidal termination of the chancel derived great beauty from its extreme simplicity, and the ridge of the roof ended with a delicate iron cross. The clerestory windows of the apse were of two lights, incorporating geometrical tracery. The vestry windows, in the walls of the apparent aisles below, were square headed and of three lights. The details of the eaves matched those of the body of the church. Much of the external beauty of the apse was derived from the semi-circular walls, which were more graceful than the segmental apsidal terminations used in many later Hull churches of this type. The general appearance of the whole building was one of restraint and simplicity, and the almost complete absence of buttresses was interesting.

Street also designed the vicarage to All Saints' church (215), whose elevation was decidedly more functional in appearance. The chimney stacks were the most carefully detailed part of the exterior. The panelled entrance hall had a slightly Jacobean flavour. Both the church and the vicarage were demolished in 1974.

In 1871 the first church designed by Samuel Musgrave, a local architect, was erected in Barmston Street. This was the church of St Silas (217), which, together with its adjoining vicarage, was demolished in 1969. Had the planned tower also been completed they would have formed quite an imposing group, but funds were only sufficient to meet the cost of the church itself, and the tower over the south porch only ever reached the level of the entrance doorway. The building was constructed of red stock bricks with a few stone dressings.

The general layout, though much smaller in scale, was very similar to that planned by Street at All Saints', with the principal entrance situated under the tower to the south of the nave aisle (223). The church was a very cheap building, and the tower would no doubt have been its finest and most expensive feature. The illustration (XLII) shows the design as it would have appeared had it been completed. The chancel ended with an apse, as at All Saints', although here the nave and chancel were under separate roofs. The chancel apse was not circular but segmental, like most church apses in Hull. The windows to the chancel had plate tracery and the aisle windows were simple lancets, two to each bay. The clerestory windows were circular and ornamented with a series of stone cusps.

The west elevation of the building had a simple entrance doorway surmounted by two rather unhappily placed two-light windows, which formed the main means of lighting the nave. In the gable was a circular window filled with plate tracery. The aisles were strengthened by buttresses and the base of the tower was also strengthened by low, broad buttresses. The steeple was very reminiscent of Street's work, although the lower part of the tower was simply typical of the period.

Part of the adjoining vicarage is also shown on the illustration (XLII); although clearly intended to be rather fine, the building as finally erected was very dull and uninteresting.

In 1874 Musgrave designed Latimer Congregational chapel in Williamson Street (222), not a particularly beautiful building, and now demolished. It was almost entirely of brick and was interesting for having a similar, although less beautiful, tower and steeple to that proposed for St Silas's. The base of the tower was abutted in a similar way by short, broad buttresses.

In 1873 Musgrave designed St Barnabas' church (220) on Hessle Road, at the corner of the Boulevard, which was closed in 1970 and subsequently demolished. This was indeed his finest work; although much smaller than All Saints', it cost only £1,000 less and internally greatly resembled Street's work. The building, which was constructed of red stock bricks and cut stone dressings, was in the Early English style.

The nave of the church was of five bays and flanked by aisles half its width. The chancel, which was placed under a separate roof, ended with a semi-circular apse similar to, but internally more beautiful than, that at All Saints'. The nave clerestory was lit by two small lancets over each bay. The aisles were also lighted by two lancets to each bay. The chancel was lit by nine clerestory windows and the nave, as at All Saints', was lit by three large windows in the west gable of the

214 – St Matthew's – View from the West

215 – All Saints' Vicarage

PLATE XLII – Church of St Silas, Barmston Street, 1871. architect: samuel musgrave

PLATE XLIII – CHURCH OF ALL SAINTS, MARGARET STREET.
DESIGN FOR THE PROPOSED "WALSHAM MEMORIAL" TOWER. ARCHITECT: S. MUSGRAVE

216 – ALL SAINTS' – VIEW FROM THE SOUTH-WEST

217 – ST SILAS'S – VIEW FROM THE SOUTH-WEST

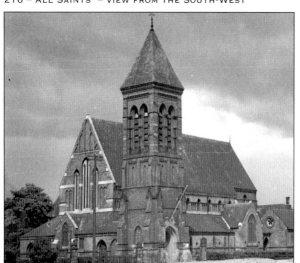

building. Only the west front was buttressed. Over the west doorway was a gable surmounted by a belfry, pierced in its lower stages by a large centre lancet. There was a small porch on the north side of the church.

The interior of the church was very beautiful. The octagonal piers supporting the arcades had capitals and bases very similar in design to All Saints' (237), as were the stone pendants surmounting the capitals. The arches of the arcades were picked out with decorative brickwork, and the chancel arch (247) was particularly fine, springing from a corbelled shaft. Above this arch was a circular motif picked out in darker bricks and bearing a cross in the centre. The arcades were surmounted by a moulding from which sprang the stone corbels supporting the main curved timbers of the roof.

The roof (242) was much better than that at All Saints', the absence of any large metal ties at the base of the roof giving an increased effect of height. The clerestory windows were paired under a decorative brick arch with splayed reveals (237).

The chancel (219) was the most beautiful part of the interior. The roof sprang from a timber cornice and was plastered, as at All Saints' (247). The clerestory lights were divided by slender stone shafts on delicate stone bases and capitals surmounted by stone pendants supporting decorative brick arches (219). The altar table was backed by a stone reredos decorated with geometrical tracery, lancets, trefoils and quatrefoils. The walls of the apse on either side of the reredos were decorated with coloured tiles forming a pattern of arches and other decorative motifs. The choir stalls were interesting and quite well carved for the time. The organ was located on the north of the chancel, as at All Saints'.

The large brass chandelier (247) was well placed, suspended from the chancel arch. The inner order of the chancel arch, in stone, was decorated in gilt lettering with the words 'Let Everything That Hath Breath Praise The Lord', and the three central lancets of the chancel apse were surmounted by the words 'Holy, Holy, Holy'.

In contrast with the richness of the chancel, the nave pews (232) were simple in design, better than those at All Saints', and the aisles as well as the nave were furnished with seating. The stone font (252) was an interesting example in the style of Street. The interior of the building was very pleasing and comfortable, and the design as a whole was very competent, making it one of Musgrave's finest works.

In 1877 Musgrave designed Hessle Road Congregational chapel (221), at the comer of Strickland Street, which was very similar in exterior treatment to St Barnabas'. The building was of red stock bricks and cut stone dressings and was quite impressive, despite the absence of a tower or steeple. Here Musgrave used plate tracery extensively, and the large wheel window over the main entrance was the most attractive feature of the building. The front buttresses were very bold and were topped by large pinnacles. The stone copings of the aisles terminated with carved stone eagles. The building was a good example of Nonconformist church architecture in this period and showed that by this time the Nonconformists were also favouring the Gothic style.

The original interior was completely altered in the early 1950s to form a theatre, and the building was later used as a warehouse. It had been demolished by 1964.

In 1883 Musgrave was commissioned to design the Walsham Memorial Tower, to complete Street's design for All Saints'. Musgrave's design (XLIII) was very competent and in keeping with the existing building; details were published in *The Builder* in 1884. The tower was tall and well proportioned and surmounted by a steeple. The whole would have contrasted well with the existing lofty roof of Street's nave. But once more insufficient money was forthcoming, and the design had to be amended and reduced considerably in height.

The tower as eventually built (212) appeared very stumpy and was almost dwarfed by the huge mass of Street's church beyond (216). The upper stages closely resembled the work of Street, but the lower part was more obviously a design by Musgrave. The short, wide buttresses so favoured by Musgrave had here an adverse effect on the apparent height of the tower; they did not occur on the original design and the amended design would have seemed loftier without them. The tower was demolished shortly after the church in 1974.

In due course Musgrave went into partnership with W. H. Bingley, and together they designed one of their last and most interesting buildings, the Victoria Hospital for Sick Children (224), built in Park Street in 1891. Externally this is one of Hull's most interesting Gothic Revival buildings. It is remarkable for its similarity in style and massing to the elevation of the Law Courts in London, which had been designed by Street some years earlier. The building is constructed of red stock bricks with cut stone dressings but is, of course, on a much smaller scale than the Law Courts. The principal upper windows display plate tracery (225), and the tower at the north end of the elevation is very similar to the tower of the Law Courts. The central entrance (225) is well designed; the flanking turrets terminating in pinnacles are smaller than those of the Law Courts.

This building, more than any of Musgrave's other designs, shows clearly how much he was influenced by the work of Street, to the extent of being his most ardent follower in Hull. However, although primarily a Gothicist, Musgrave was also an exponent of eclecticism and designed Queen's Road and Brunswick Wesleyan chapel in the classical manner.

218 – All Saints' – View of Chancel

219 – St Barnabas' – Chancel

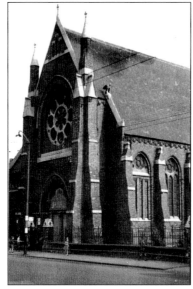

221 – Hessle Road Congregational Chapel

220 – St Barnabas' – General View

222 – Latimer Congregational Chapel

223 – St Silas's – South Porch

225 – Children's Hospital– Main Entrance

224 – Victoria Hospital for Sick Children, Park Street

In 1870, following an architectural competition, St Matthew's church (214), on Anlaby Road, at the corner of the Boulevard, was erected to the designs of Adams and Kelly. This is the only church in this group to be faced with white stock bricks, the first since St James's in 1830. The white bricks are relieved with horizontal bands of red bricks, and the tracery, copings and other external details are of stone. The building consists of a nave of six bays with wide north and south aisles. The chancel is under a separate, lower roof and terminates with a segmental apse of three bays. At the eastern end of the north aisle is a lofty tower surmounted by a broach spire built almost entirely of white stock bricks. The tower also abuts the northern side of the chancel. The building displays some of the finest plate tracery in the city, the west window being a particularly interesting, although not altogether happy design, with a large open area in the centre of the circular portion.

Internally, the church is plastered and is the only one of this group which is so treated; the remainder are faced with brickwork. The general appearance of the interior is French in character (233); no doubt the result of the three years spent by Kelly in Street's office.

The nave has a timber barrelled roof (243), which springs from a simple timber wallplate with thin metal ties between each bay. The rather heavy arcading is supported by cylindrical stone columns which have immense stone bases rising above the pews (238). The square capitals are decorated with carved leaves and have a very French appearance. The arches of the arcades are formed in red brickwork and have a moulded brick hoodmould. At the points where the hoodmoulds intersect, there are projecting heads and shoulders of various figures executed in terracotta. A horizontal stone moulding runs above the arcades at the level from which the chancel arch springs. Each bay of the nave is surmounted by three grouped lancet windows (238). The chancel arch is formed of brickwork and is of two orders (248), the inner order being supported by a single cylindrical stone shaft at each side with a square capital decorated with carved leaves.

The chancel roof is of timber springing from a deep timber cornice. A horizontal stone moulding continues round the chancel at the level from which spring the arches of the windows. From this moulding spring corbels with carved figures supporting slender cylindrical stone shafts which, in turn, support the principal ribs of the roof. The roof cornice to the three bays of the apse bears the words 'Holy, Holy, Holy' in gilt. The organ is situated under the tower and is exposed by two arches, one on the north of the chancel and the other at the east end of the north aisle. The three windows of the chancel apse are each of three lights and terminate with a circular window, an arrangement similar, though taller in proportion, to the apse windows of Street's St James the Less, Westminster.

The aisle windows are also each of three lights surmounted by a central circular window flanked by a trefoil at each side. The west walls of the aisles are pierced by windows each of two lights surmounted by a quatrefoil.

The west front of the nave has buttresses of simple design and the bays of the aisles also are buttressed. The tower (214), of three stages, is flanked by two buttresses on each elevation. The second stage is pierced by four decorative lancets. The belfry stage above has two lancets to each elevation, each surmounted by a quatrefoil and the openings filled with timber slats. The broach spire is constructed of white stock bricks and has horizontal double decorative bands of red brickwork at intervals. Each side of the spire is ornamented at the bottom with a gabled stone window. The spire terminates with a stone finial, which is surmounted by a delicate wrought iron cross. The building as a whole is quite pleasing, and the large windows of the aisles, nave and chancel, together with the plastered walls, make it the lightest church of its type in Hull.

A Bradford architect, Edward Simpson, was responsible for the design of two churches, St Jude's and St Thomas's, which are typical of their time and also show the influence of Street and his contemporaries.

St Jude's, on Spring Bank (230), erected in 1874, but demolished in 1973, was the first of these. It was a large red brick building with a steeply pitched roof to the nave, and wide aisles with low pitched roofs, very reminiscent of All Saints'. The chancel was under a separate roof and its square east end was pierced by three lancets. The building, which was in the Early English style, had no buttresses to its nave aisles and chancel; the only examples abutted the west gable and terminated in stunted square pinnacles.

The nave was of six bays, and the clerestories and aisles were lit by small lancet windows, two to each bay. The interior, in general, was more like All Saints' than any of the preceding churches, but it was very simply detailed. It was very dark since the principal means of natural lighting was the large, traceried circular window in the west gable. The western end of the north aisle was also lit by a circular window. The principal entrance was the north aisle porch, and there was also an entrance porch formed between excessively projecting buttresses at the west end. Stone was only used here for copings and for the tracery of the large circular window at the west end.

St John's, Newington (228), in St George's Road, was erected 1876-8 to the designs of Smith and Brodrick; it has since been demolished. The walls of the nave were plastered originally (234), the arches of the arcades and the aisle walls being of brick. Canon Tardrew, the former incumbent, redecorated the whole of the interior, including the brickwork. He also painted the pews of the church green.

The interior (234) was very similar to that of St

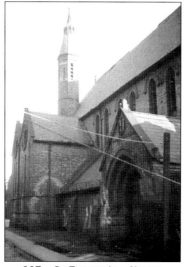

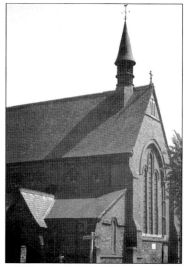

226 – St Thomas's – Detail of Apse

227 – St Thomas's – North Elevation

228 – St John's, Newington – View from North West

229 – St Thomas's – Exterior of Nave

230 – St Jude's Church, Spring Bank

Comparative Interiors Looking East

231 All Saints

232 – St Barnabas'

233 – St Matthew's

234 – St John's, Newington

235 – St Thomas's

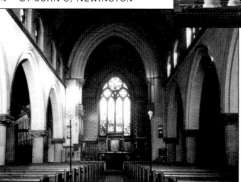

Matthew's, and the cylindrical stone columns (239) had square stone capitals decorated with carved foliage. The arches were formed of brickwork. A stone cornice ran above the arcades, and the clerestory was composed of circular windows with five cusps which had square surrounds to the interior and flat arched heads. There were two of these windows to each bay. Between the clerestory windows were projecting stone corbels which supported the simple roof trusses (244). The chancel arch (249) was of three orders; the inner order supported on a corbelled cylindrical shaft on either side, each with a capital decorated with carved foliage. The roof of the chancel was the same as that of the nave and the trusses were painted. The geometrical east window was the best feature of the interior; it was of four lights and of pleasing design. The organ was sited in the usual place on the north side of the chancel. The pulpit (253) was of stone and very similar in design to that of All Saints'.

Whilst the church was very plain and simple outside, it had a surprisingly pleasing interior and was a good example of a well-designed, cheap church building, much better than St Jude's.

St Thomas's (227), erected in Campbell Street in 1882, was the more interesting of Simpson's two churches. Like St Jude's, St Thomas's was a very cheap building. It was badly shaken in both World Wars and was demolished in the 1950s. It was primarily of interest for the way in which it was planned to suit a very awkward and restricted site. Here, Simpson succeeded in giving the church the correct east-west orientation. In east Hull – St Peter's, Drypool, and St Mark's apart – this was seldom the case.

The church comprised a nave of six bays with north and south transepts and aisles, and a chancel terminating with a segmental apse (226). The chancel and nave were under the same roof, as at All Saints', and the chancel was narrower than the nave. The apse faced on to the road, and the small steeple was placed on the northern side of the apse (227), forming a focal point from the Anlaby Road approach to the church.

The west and south sides of the site were entirely built up to clerestory level, and the main entrance was in the north aisle (227), approached from a small terrace adjacent to Campbell Street. The vestry entrance was in Campbell Street, on the south side of the apse. Owing to the proximity of the adjoining property, the north and south aisles had no windows, and the west gable was lighted by three large lancets at clerestory level (229). The church was in the Early English style.

The interior walls of the building were plastered throughout (235). The stone piers supporting the arcades were alternately circular and segmental. They had high bases and deep capitals, and their general appearance was one of stumpiness (240). Natural lighting was provided only by the windows at clerestory level; a very tall clerestory (245) had therefore been provided, almost as high above the cornice surmounting the arcading as was the arcading itself. The arches of the arcades had thus been kept as low as possible, giving the stumpy appearance. The transepts were each approached by two well-proportioned arches (235) which extended to the height of the tops of the clerestory windows. The arches to both transepts were divided by a free-standing, square moulded stone column, with a heavy base and rather clumsily detailed capital. The arch was of two orders; the outer order was supported on the walls on either side, while the inner order was supported on each side by a slender cylindrical shaft in four sections, having a high base and a simply moulded capital. The arches of the nave arcades and the chancel arch were all formed in plaster, originally treated to imitate stone.

The curious roof construction of the nave (245) was an unusual feature, unique amongst churches of this type in Hull. It consisted of a series of principal timber 'scissor' trusses between each bay, and smaller intermediate trusses at the centre of each bay. The principal trusses had curved members to their undersides and a semi-circular curved member at the apex. The main trusses were supported by stone corbels which projected from the cornice surmounting the nave arcades. There is evidence that these corbels were originally carried by cylindrical shafts supported by smaller brackets between the arcade arches. The intermediate trusses sprang from corbels above the lancet windows; they were much simpler in design and were entirely composed of straight pieces of timber.

The roof of the chancel apse was similar to, though not as good as, the chancel roof of St Matthew's. As the chancel was under the same roof as the nave, but narrower in width, the side walls were higher. The chancel was lighted at clerestory level by five tall and well-proportioned lancet windows, each of two lights surmounted by a circular light. The communion rails were of a delicate design carried out in iron. Seating was provided in both the body of the church and in the aisles.

Externally, the structure was rather plain and was constructed of red stock bricks with a few stone dressings. The west gable was pierced by three lancets grouped under a large decorative brick arch (229), similar to the west gable of St John's, St George's Road. The buttresses abutting the west gable were similar in design to those of St Jude's. The east end of the main roof ridge was ornamented with decorative wrought iron cresting. The small octagonal brick belfry was surmounted by a small spire roofed with tiles.

These three churches – St Jude's, St Thomas's and St John's – were essentially very cheap buildings. Yet they were all quite different, and internally had many points of interest both in construction and design. St Jude's was strongly influenced by Street's All Saints', but was a very dreary and uninspired copy. The interior of St

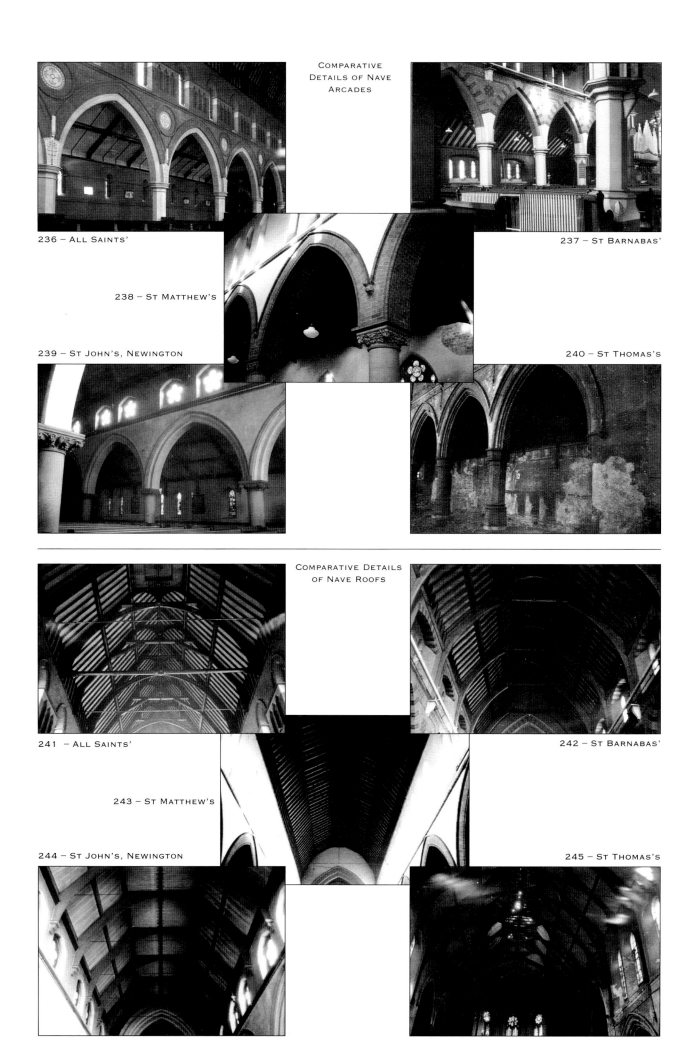

COMPARATIVE
DETAILS OF NAVE
ARCADES

236 – ALL SAINTS'

237 – ST BARNABAS'

238 – ST MATTHEW'S

239 – ST JOHN'S, NEWINGTON

240 – ST THOMAS'S

COMPARATIVE DETAILS
OF NAVE ROOFS

241 – ALL SAINTS'

242 – ST BARNABAS'

243 – ST MATTHEW'S

244 – ST JOHN'S, NEWINGTON

245 – ST THOMAS'S

John's was no doubt partly inspired by St Matthew's, and had a certain French appearance in its arcading. St Thomas's was by far the most original of the three and showed that Simpson in particular, had the ability to adapt his designs well to an awkward site. Whilst in line with previous styles, it was not directly influenced by any of the earlier churches erected in Hull.

Samuel Musgrave usually built a better type of church than Simpson and was very much influenced by the work of Street. St Barnabas', Musgrave's finest church in Hull, was very much in the Street style. Although much smaller than All Saints', it was on the whole more pleasing. St Matthew's is a fine example of the church architecture of the period and also shows Street's influence, although its use of white stock bricks was not then general for Hull churches.

The School Board Gothic Style

Between 1870 and 1880 a number of Board Schools were erected in the Gothic style, mainly to the designs of William Botterill. The new Grammar School buildings (256) were erected slightly later in Leicester Street, to the designs of Smith and Brodrick.

Among the first of these Board Schools was Williamson Street (255), designed in 1874 by William Botterill. It had rather a stark and unfriendly appearance, with its red stock bricks and Welsh slated roofs. The tower was the most interesting feature, with three lancet windows at the ground-floor level, surmounted by the arms of the town, the date of erection and the words 'Board School'. The upper stage of the tower accommodated the bell and had slatted lancet windows on each side. The tower terminated with an octagonal steeple. The single-storey building was essentially a symmetrical composition, with the belfry tower stuck on at the southern end to make it asymmetrical. The school was demolished 1993-4.

In 1877 Botterill designed Fountain Road Board School (257), on the whole a more pleasing building than Williamson Street. This school, which has since been demolished, accommodated boys, girls and infants, and was arranged in three separate sections, each with its own playground (XLIV). The single-storey wing at the east end accommodated the infants' school, while the ground floor of the two-storey block accommodated the girls' school, with the boys' school on the floor above. Botterill made use of plate tracery for the principal gable windows.

In 1878 he designed Osborne Street Schools (258), also now demolished, on much the same lines as Fountain Road. Here a more interesting form of plate tracery was used in the gable window surmounting the main entrance. In 1879 Constable Street Board School (254) was erected, of which only small parts now survive. It was typical of many of Botterill's later Board Schools in this style. The building was symmetrical about the central entrance (the entrance on the left of the illustration). This single-storey building, of red stock bricks with cut stone dressings and slated roofs, comprised the infants' school in the centre, and the boys' and girls' schools to either side. The playgrounds were located behind the buildings, which fronted directly on to the street. All these schools were surmounted by *flèches*, but on the whole were rather dull.

In 1881 William Freeman designed St George's Road Board School on similar lines. Rather better was Musgrave's Sir Henry Cooper Board School, Bean Street, erected in 1876, and now demolished. It was a single-storey building of considerable length fronting on to the street. The infants' entrance (260) formed the centre of the symmetrical design and was backed by the gable of the hall roof, which was surmounted by a belfry similar to the one at St Barnabas' church. The infants' section was flanked on either side by the boys' and girls' schools. The building, of red stock bricks with stone dressings, had windows of a simple Gothic character; only the gable window of the hall had plate tracery. The chimneys were carefully detailed, and the upper part of the belfry was of stone surmounted by a delicate finial. The two wings of the building were surmounted by belfry *flèches*. The large number of windows of varying sizes and the number of small pieces of stone tended to give the building a rather spotted appearance. However, the exterior as a whole was very exciting and a great improvement on many Board Schools of this type.

Botterill's Blundell Street School (259, 261) of 1878 also shows a little more vitality in its design. Red stock bricks, cut stone dressings and slated roofs were again used. The general arrangement is that of Fountain Road, but the elevational treatment is more powerful and determined. The gable of the infants' school (259) has two windows of three lights, surmounted by circular windows. The gable is pierced by a circular window, and all three windows are interesting examples of plate tracery. The boys' and girls' schools are in a two-storey block, north of the infants' school, and the principal entrance is surmounted by a low tower terminating with a pointed roof. The tower (261) terminates with a decorative stone cornice and has an open, gabled stone arch at the front. The first-floor gable window of this block, composed of four lights surmounted by three circular windows, is one of the best examples of School Board plate tracery in Hull.

In 1892 the new Grammar School buildings were erected in Leicester Street (256), to the designs of Smith and Brodrick, in red stock bricks with cut stone dressings and slated roofs. The assembly hall is the low gabled building to the left of the entrance and the formrooms are located on the right-hand

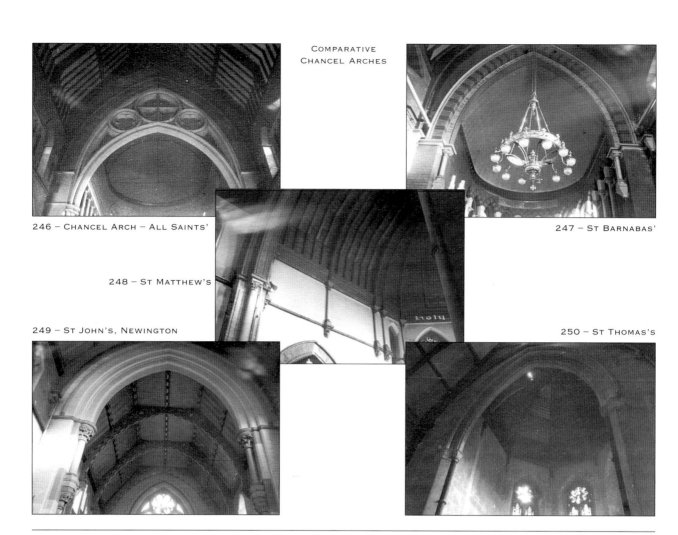

246 – CHANCEL ARCH – ALL SAINTS'

247 – ST BARNABAS'

248 – ST MATTHEW'S

249 – ST JOHN'S, NEWINGTON

250 – ST THOMAS'S

251 – PULPIT – ALL SAINTS'

252 – PULPIT – ST BARNABAS'

253 – FONT – ST JOHN'S, NEWINGTON.

side. The building is primarily a late example of School Board Gothic and the windows have features in the Jacobean style which was later to become popular. The buildings are architecturally rather poor and not of the standard to be expected of such an ancient foundation as Hull Grammar School.

The Geometrical Revival

Between 1861 and 1863 George Gilbert Scott was engaged to carry out the restoration of St Mary's Church in Lowgate (263). In 1850 Scott had published his *Plea for the Faithful Restoration of our Ancient Churches*, which sets out clearly the folly of much that was going on at the time, giving some wise advice on the subject. Scott, however, failed to take his own counsel, either then or later.

Comparing the two plates of St Mary's (XI, XLV) shows that Scott, far from carefully restoring the church, in fact altered its external appearance beyond recognition. By the time he had finished, St Mary's appeared as a typical Victorian church, with its profusion of heavy, ornate pinnacles. He completely encased the brick and stone tower with stonework to a new design bearing no relation whatsoever to the original. It is not, however, difficult to detect its origins; it is a reasonably good copy of the tower of Magdalen College, Oxford.

By this time Lowgate was becoming a busy thoroughfare due to commercial expansion in the area. Scott therefore formed an archway under the tower for the use of pedestrians. He added a new south aisle to the existing south aisle, and also a small south porch. The style of the new extensions is primarily Perpendicular in character, presumably to harmonise with the clerestory windows of the nave, the only windows he did not alter. The whole of the exterior of the building, apart from the clerestories of the nave, was then clothed in a new stone face, giving the building its present appearance. Internally, the church was left pretty much in its original state. However, the nave roof, which was throughout of rough timber with a flat plaster ceiling, was overlaid with pitch pine, moulded and ornamented to form the roof we see today.

In 1868 Scott also designed the new St Mary's Vicarage (264), now St Mary's Court. It is a large, four-storey brick building with stone dressings, the chief feature being the large oriel window to the first floor. The building as a whole is not particularly exciting and is very plain compared with his work on St Mary's church. It is, however, a much more interesting building than All Saints' Vicarage, designed by Street.

In 1860 the foundation stone was laid of Beverley Road Wesleyan chapel, which was designed by William Botterill in the Decorated Gothic style (XLVI), and opened in 1862. The building, which had a frontage to Beverley Road of 112 feet and stood back 45 feet from the road, was destroyed by fire in the early 1950s. All the external walls were faced with the best Wallingfen white stock bricks, and the ornamented masonry and other dressings were of Brodsworth stone.

The Beverley Road elevation was divided by buttresses into three spaces, each having an arched entrance doorway, with columns of red Mansfield stone and floriated capitals. On each side of the central doorway was a two-light window, whose hood mouldings were united with those of the doorway and rose triangularly from carved terminations to form three small gables with finials. Above the central doorway was a five-light mullioned window, with rich tracery in the head, continuing up into the roof gable. Above each of the side doorways was a two-light window. Octagonal pinnacles, with crocketed tops, rose from the offsets of the principal buttresses, and square pinnacles from the heads of the side buttresses. The gable was surmounted by an octagonal turret with two stages of arches and a small spire; the projection in front of the face of the wall rested upon a moulded and carved corbel. The front of the chapel had a wing on each side for the gallery staircase, and the side elevations of the building were divided by bold, receding buttresses into bays with two tiers of traceried windows on account of the galleries.

This building was a good example of the basic requirements of a Nonconformist church treated in the Gothic style. It was the first Nonconformist church to be erected in Hull in this style and shows how well Botterill used it and adapted it to his requirements. The front of the building comprises a very wide gable, but it is so well handled that it avoids any appearance of weakness or bad proportion. The building as a whole was a very competent design.

In 1871, Joseph Wright designed Bourne Primitive Methodist chapel (267) on Anlaby Road, now demolished. Like Wright's earlier chapels, it was sited at a junction – here Bean Street and Anlaby Road – to form a focal point terminating the view at the end of a street. His design may have been inspired by Botterill's earlier Beverley Road chapel, which it resembled in many ways. Wright's two earlier chapels, which were both very fine, had a definite French Renaissance flavour about them. Here he decided to try his hand at the Gothic style, but with little success.

The materials used were those of Beverley Road chapel and the general proportion was similar, but here the elevation looked very weak and badly proportioned. The general arrangement of the units on the front was the same, although here the gallery staircases were contained within the main block. In Botterill's design the buttresses were powerful enough to reduce the apparent width of the gable. Here they were extremely weak and might just as well have been omitted. In the Beverley Road design the large window over the central porch echoed the well-proportioned centre bay. Here the window

254 – Board Schools – Constable Street

255 – Board Schools – Williamson Street

256 – Grammar School, Leicester Street

257 – Board Schools – Fountain Road

258 – Board Schools – Osborne Street

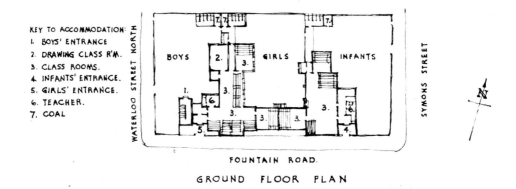

KEY TO ACCOMMODATION:
1. BOYS' ENTRANCE
2. DRAWING CLASS R'M.
3. CLASS ROOMS.
4. INFANTS' ENTRANCE.
5. GIRLS' ENTRANCE.
6. TEACHER.
7. COAL

GROUND FLOOR PLAN

PLATE XLIV – FOUNTAIN ROAD BOARD SCHOOLS, 1876. ARCHITECT: WILLIAM BOTTERILL

BOARD SCHOOLS

259 – BLUNDELL
STREET

260 – SIR HENRY
COOPER, BEAN
STREET

261 – BLUNDELL
STREET

262 – SIR HENRY
COOPER, BEAN
STREET

PLATE XLV – ST MARY'S CHURCH, LOWGATE, AFTER EXTENSION AND RESTORATION BY SIR GEORGE GILBERT SCOTT, 1860-3.

PLATE XLVI – Beverley Road Wesleyan Chapel, 1860. architect: William Botterill

PLATE XLVII – Wycliffe Congregational Chapel, 1865. architect: W. H. Kitching

263 – St Mary's, Lowgate

264 – St Mary's Vicarage

265 – Stepney Methodist New Connexion Chapel

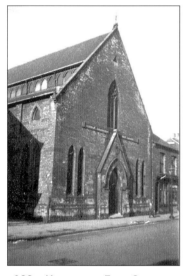

266 – Methodist Free Church, Campbell Street

270 – Unitarian Church – Detail of Front

267 – Bourne Methodist Chapel, Anlaby Road

268 – St Andrew's Church, Holderness Road

269 – Unitarian Church, Park Street

echoed the proportion of the whole elevation and thus emphasised its bad proportions. The details of the doorways and windows were well executed, but the whole lacked the vigour and vitality so apparent in Botterill's design.

In 1865 Wycliffe Congregational chapel (XLVII) was erected on Anlaby Road, at the corner of Campbell Street, to the designs of William Kitching. The building, which formed a curious little group from the exterior, was demolished in 1939.

It comprised a nave with aisles, transepts and a tower with a spire. The building was in the late Early English style and was faced with white stock bricks with cut stone dressings. One of the most interesting features of the building was the replacement of orthodox stone piers by light iron columns with wrought iron foliated capitals which supported the interesting timber roof construction. The roof was open to the collar beam and from the caps of the columns sprang, both longitudinally and transversely across the nave, moulded timber ribs.

In 1866 Kitching designed the Methodist Free church in Campbell Street (266), now demolished. It was a very simple design. The front of the building, like Bourne Methodist church, was badly proportioned, being excessive in width for its height. The simple entrance portico was slightly projected and flanked by two small lancets. The doorway was surmounted by a window containing Geometrical tracery, which gave the impression that it had been rather squashed together to make it fit. On account of the proximity of the adjoining buildings, a shallow clerestory formed in timber was concealed behind the front gable, which was partly false.

In 1881 Kitching designed the Unitarian church (269), in Park Street, demolished c.1976. This was an extraordinary example of late Early English Gothic. The projecting porches flanked the front gable of the nave and terminated the side aisles. The front of the church faced east, and at the northeast corner was a short buttressed tower (270), surmounted by an octagonal spire. The tower and spire, a confusion of odd shapes and bits and pieces, were very badly designed. The body of the church, which was of six bays, had double lancets to the aisle bays, and there was a timber clerestory similar to that at Campbell Street chapel.

Stepney New Connexion Methodist chapel, Beverley Road (265), was built in 1869, to the designs of William Hill, of Leeds. An interesting example of a small church of this period, it has since been demolished and replaced by a Kwik Save supermarket. It was similar to Kitching's work but was more restrained. In the late Early English style, it was constructed of white stock bricks with ornamental patterned red brickwork and cut stone dressings. The double entrance porches had arches supported by three cylindrical columns with carved foliated capitals. The entrances were surmounted by a group of three traceried windows. The belfry windows of the tower were filled with ornamental cast iron grills. The eaves projection of the tower was rather excessive for the height and size of the tower and spire.

The church of St John the Evangelist, Prospect Street, was erected in 1866, on the site of the present Central Library, to the designs of Alexander Gough. The church, in the late Early English style, was faced with Bradford stone (rockfaced), with Steetley limestone dressings; lined in the interior with brick; and plastered. The building comprised a nave with side aisles, an apsidal chancel with a vestry on one side and an organ chamber on the other, north and south transepts, and a tower surmounted by a spire on the south side of the nave. The nave and chancel had a clerestory pierced with trefoil-shaped lights. The principal entrance was in the west front. This front was gabled and contained a large circular or 'rose' window, with very elaborate tracery. Each side of the body of the church was in six gabled bays and contained a doorway, four three-light windows, one window of two lights and a rose window over each entrance. The tower, which was in five stages, was 66 feet in height, and was surmounted by a spire 58 feet in height.

Many churches of the last quarter of the 19th century are entirely nondescript; red brick suburban churches which have no merit and need no description.

This is certainly the case of St Andrew's (268), erected in 1878 on Holderness Road, at the corner of Abbey Street, and demolished in 1984. A poor example of the work of Adams and Kelly, it was in the late Early English style and bears no comparison with their earlier St Matthew's. Its chief point of interest was that it was one of those churches in East Hull which were incorrectly orientated, the usual west gable here facing north.

CHAPTER VIII

THE ELIZABETHAN AND JACOBEAN REVIVALS

The effect of the Elizabethan and Jacobean revivals on the architecture of Hull was comparatively slight, for only four buildings sympathetic to the original Elizabethan or Jacobean styles were erected. However, they are all buildings of a high standard architecturally.

Holderness House (271) was erected in 1838 to the designs of James Clephan, a London architect. Holderness House, then well out in the country, was originally the seat of Boswell Middleton Jalland. In more recent times it was the home of T. R. Ferens, a local benefactor, who left it on his death to Hull Corporation as a retirement home.

The house, which is very large and in the Elizabethan style, is constructed of white stock bricks with cut stone dressings and has slate roofs. The principal or south-west front of the mansion (271) exhibits a centre with gabled projecting sides, in which are four fine bay windows with stone mullions and transoms. The south-east front (272) is also very fine, and the centre gable projects slightly beyond the general face of the building. Both elevations have a raised terrace in front of them, upon which the ground-floor windows open. On the north-west side is a square tower, which contains the entrance (273), approached by a large flight of steps. The entrance hall is stately and spacious, and the principal apartments are finely proportioned. The grand staircase is very fine and its vestibule is supported by Ionic columns.

Within its well-wooded precinct, the grounds and mansion form one of the most beautiful aspects in Hull today; adequately screened from the roar of the traffic in the now busy town surrounding it, with its mellowed and creeper covered walls, the house has an air of tranquility and peace very fitting for a retirement home.

In 1865 Hull Seamen's and General Orphan Asylum (XLVIII) was erected on Spring Bank to the designs of T. H. Wyatt, the London architect. The building, four storeys in height and in the Elizabethan style, was constructed of red brick with cut stone dressings. There was a frontage on Spring Bank of 120 feet. The building stood 50 feet from the roadway and was raised for the purpose of providing a basement storey. It was later renamed Government Buildings and used for many years as government offices, before being demolished in 1989.

Originally, the basement floor contained the work rooms, kitchens and other offices. The ground floor housed schoolrooms, classrooms for both sexes, the matron's room, waiting rooms, stores and the refectory. The first floor contained bedrooms for both sexes, sick wards, and the matron's room in the centre. The attic storey contained other dormitories, infirmary and servants' bedrooms. There was a main staircase in the centre of the building and one at each end, constructed in towers, for the use of the orphans.

The elevations of the building were very pleasant and the main entrance was approached by a flight of steps. The ends of the front elevation terminated with slightly projecting gables.

The building was subsequently greatly extended by Smith and Brodrick in perfect accord with the original design. Much of the eastern extension shown in (XLVIII) was destroyed in the Second World War, although the fine secondary side entrance survived.

In 1890 the College of Commerce (275), originally the Girls' Central Secondary School, now Brunswick House, was erected in Brunswick Avenue to the designs of Botterill and Bilson. The Brunswick Avenue elevation, although very small, is carried out with red brick and stone dressings in the Jacobean style, and is very pleasing. It is a later development of Bilson's School Board style, which is discussed more fully in the next chapter.

In 1891, following an open architectural competition, Hymers College (277) was erected, to the designs of John Bilson. Standing in one of Hull's most beautiful settings, Bilson's original building and the later additions (276) together form an imposing pile.

Bilson's original design is illustrated (XLIX, LI); the general arrangement of the plan followed the instructions prepared by the assessor. Two floors of eight classrooms each are grouped around a central hall, every classroom being entered directly from the hall or from the galleries which surround it on three sides. The administrative offices are placed beneath the hall windows on the fourth side, and the principal staircase is directly opposite the main entrance. This arrangement allowed the headmaster's and porter's rooms to command the entire hall with its entrances and staircases. The original design provided cloakrooms for each classroom, but, instead, cloak-lockers were placed around the hall, following the system adopted at St Paul's School. The dining hall, with its kitchen, offices and a porter's house, was shown in a separate block connected with the main building by a covered way, but this too was not realised.

The ground-floor plan as it was actually carried out (L) shows little change from the original plan. The music room and secondary staircase were omitted from the design, making the scheme almost symmetrical.

In the original elevations, only the windows of the hall and the single-storey offices in front were of the Jacobean style. The remainder of the windows

271 – Holderness House –
West Front

272 – Holderness House –
South Front

273 – Holderness House –
Main Entrance

275 – College of Commerce

274 – Hymers College –
Porter's Lodge

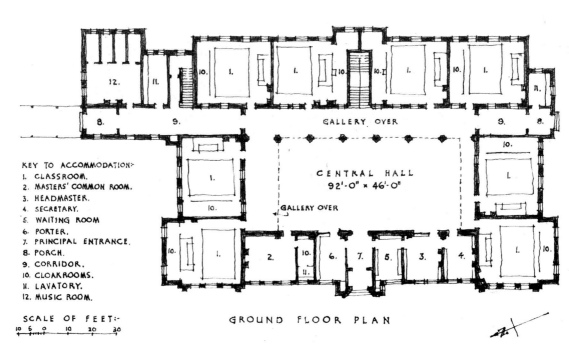

KEY TO ACCOMMODATION:-
1. CLASSROOM.
2. MASTERS' COMMON ROOM.
3. HEADMASTER.
4. SECRETARY.
5. WAITING ROOM.
6. PORTER.
7. PRINCIPAL ENTRANCE.
8. PORCH.
9. CORRIDOR.
10. CLOAKROOMS.
11. LAVATORY.
12. MUSIC ROOM.

SCALE OF FEET:-
10 5 0   10   20   30

GALLERY OVER

CENTRAL HALL
92'-0" x 46'-0"

GALLERY OVER

GROUND FLOOR PLAN

PLATE XLIX – First Premiated design for Hymers College. architect: john bilson.

BUILDING AFTER BEING EXTENDED BY SMITH AND BRODRICK.

ORIGINAL BUILDING DESIGNED BY T. H. WYATT, 1865

PLATE XLVIII − HULL SEAMEN'S AND GENERAL ORPHAN ASYLUM, SPRING BANK

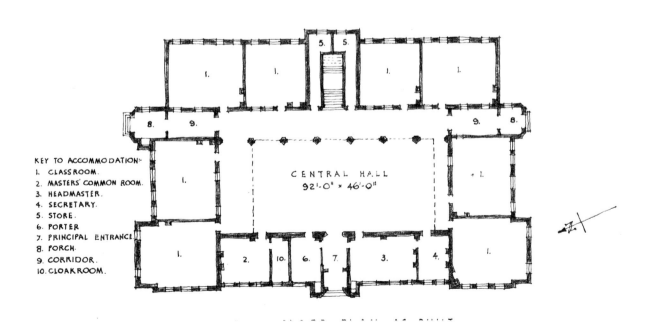

KEY TO ACCOMMODATION:
1. CLASSROOM.
2. MASTERS' COMMON ROOM.
3. HEADMASTER.
4. SECRETARY.
5. STORE.
6. PORTER.
7. PRINCIPAL ENTRANCE.
8. PORCH.
9. CORRIDOR.
10. CLOAKROOM.

CENTRAL HALL
92'-0" x 46'-0"

PLATE L − HYMERS COLLEGE 1891 - GROUND FLOOR PLAN AS BUILT

were timber framed, the style Bilson had used in many of his Board Schools. The front gables flanking the hall had buttresses similar in design to those used by Bilson on the front elevation of Stepney Schools on Beverley Road (LI). When the plans were amended, the elevations were slightly changed, and all the windows were treated in the Jacobean style, giving the building more dignity and unity. The main entrance (278) was also slightly altered in design, the fine clock tower surmounting the roof of the central hall (279) marking Bilson's supreme achievement in the design of *flèches*, discussed in more detail in the next chapter.

At the time of building, a second block to accommodate the science laboratories was already envisaged and only temporary laboratories were provided in the main building. The science building was erected shortly after the main building, the two linked at first-floor level by an archway beneath which are the entrances to both buildings. Following the First World War, the beautiful oak-panelled Memorial Hall was erected at the south end of the original block, giving the college the appearance we see today from the grounds (276). The extensions were designed by Bilson in perfect harmony with the original building.

The buildings are constructed of red brick with Ancaster stone dressings and red tiled roofs. The roof to the single-storey block in front of the hall is, however, of Westmorland slate. The exterior of the building as it appears today is in every way an admirable and beautiful conception. A comparison with the original elevational treatment shows many minor alterations, in addition to the windows, which all add up to make this Bilson's greatest achievement. He was undoubtedly a great architect and this building well displays his thorough knowledge of historical styles and his ability to adapt them to the requirements of his time.

Internally, the lofty central hall (283) is a fine example of his work. The main body of the hall is of seven bays and has a fine arcade on its eastern side, which balances the massive clerestory windows on the opposite side. The large octagonal piers (281), which soar up through the two storeys of the building, have smaller three-quarter octagonal pilasters on their inner sides, which support the brackets of the lofty, timber, Jacobean-style roof, illuminated by dormer windows. The fine roof (280) is the best timber roof of this period in the whole city. The pilasters terminate with carefully detailed capitals carved with an acanthus leaf pattern (282).

The roof brackets on the western side of the hall spring from carved stone corbels. The lower roof brackets, displaying open timberwork, terminate with fine carved pendants, which give the appearance of supporting the main transverse trusses and the intermediate longitudinal bracing trusses. The principal upper trusses are supported at their centre by large carved vertical members of Jacobean character, which rise from the principal transverse members. The timber boarded roof rises from a splayed stone cornice. The bases of the stone piers (281) to the arcade are simply but well designed, and the first-floor gallery is supported by carved stone brackets on either side of each pier, similar to but smaller than the brackets which support the western ends of the roof trusses. The arches of the arcade (282) are semi-circular, and the deep mouldings are decorated with a series of medallions and motifs, ornamented with carved foliage surrounds.

The gallery at the north end has fixed pew seating and is supported by a square, timber, Jacobean-style column at the centre. The design of the balustrading surrounding three sides of the hall is well executed and is in harmony with the rest of the interior. The main staircase (284, 285) is an interesting feature, rising in a single flight with an intermediate landing to a small gallery, from which two narrower flights with an intermediate landing continue to the first floor.

The massive stone handrails and balustrades are the most striking feature of the staircase as a whole, deriving much of their beauty from their massiveness and simplicity of detailing. The staircase gallery has a lofty pitched roof and is lit by two tall Jacobean windows of two lights which form the main feature of the east elevation.

The porter's lodge (274), situated at the entrance to the well-wooded drive leading to the college, is an excellent example of Bilson's domestic architecture. With its red brick walls, tiled roofs and tile hanging it harmonises admirably with the rest of the scheme, which is throughout of a very high architectural standard and a lasting tribute to one of Hull's leading architects of the 19th century.

276 – Hymers College – View from South West

278 – Main Entrance

279 – Detail of West Front

277 – Main Building

PLATE LI – First Premiated design for Hymers College. architect: John Bilson

280 – Hymers College Interior – Hall Roof

281 – Detail of Pier

282 – Detail of Roof

283 – Central Hall

284 – Staircase

285 –
Staircase

CHAPTER IX
THE DUTCH AND FLEMISH INFLUENCES

John Bilson was also the architect primarily responsible for the introduction of Flemish and Dutch Renaissance characteristics into many new buildings in Hull between 1880 and 1900.

On going into partnership with William Botterill in 1881, Bilson replaced him as architect to the School Board and went on to design most of Hull's new school buildings over the next 20 years. Botterill had used the Gothic style for most of his buildings, often with dreary and uninspiring results. However, Bilson's first Board School, Buckingham Street (286), 1882, had a Dutch Renaissance feel in its details, as did its successor, Westbourne Street, 1885.

In 1886 Bilson designed his first building in the Dutch Renaissance style, the Hull and Sculcoates Dispensary in Baker Street (293). The building, which is of red brick with cut stone dressings, has a fine Dutch gable and had an entrance doorway in the Flemish style. The ground floor has since been rebuilt.

In the same year he also designed Stepney Schools (291), perhaps his most pleasing Board Schools. Plate (LII) shows the ground-floor layout of the building. The requirements were similar to those at Fountain Road, but here the problem has been approached with much more imagination. Bilson made the principal two-storey block parallel to Beverley Road, thus throwing the remainder of the buildings out of line with Stepney Lane. The front elevation is terminated at each end with a slightly projecting block surmounted by a fine Dutch gable. The six centre bays of the building are abutted on the ground floor with buttresses which continue as pilasters, similar to those originally proposed for Hymers College. The centre two bays are emphasised with tall windows surmounted by small Dutch gables, and the whole design is crowned by a fine octagonal belfry of two stages, very similar in design to the clock tower later used at Hymers College.

Between 1886 and 1890 Bilson designed a number of Board Schools in Hull in the Dutch style, all constructed of red brickwork with stone dressings. Clifton Street Schools (292), erected in 1888, are similar to Stepney Schools, although they are a much cheaper job. The gables have since been altered and the belfry removed.

Malton Street School (287), 1888, is unique amongst Bilson's schools in its use of a stepped gable. It is interesting to compare this building with Sculcoates National School (XXVII), erected in 1852, an earlier example of this treatment. Malton Street shows a skilled and careful handling of the details, while the National School typifies a builder's attempt at this gable treatment.

Chiltern Street School (294, 295), erected in 1890, and now demolished, also had a number of Dutch gables, but it is the last school Bilson designed in this style which possesses the most beautiful of these. Middleton Street School (288), 1890, just off Spring Bank, is now demolished, though when partly destroyed its lovely gable still formed the focal point of the street termination.

About this time Bilson adopted the Jacobean style in his designs for the College of Commerce and Hymers College. This doubtless would have been too extravagant for any future Board Schools, so he developed a new manner embodying features of both the Dutch and Jacobean styles, which might best be described as his 'School Board' style.

Scarborough Street School (289), 1893, now demolished, was one of the first to be designed in the new style. The main gables were treated in a similar manner to those of Hymers College. The centre windows of the first-floor rooms were emphasised by tall windows projecting above the eaves and terminating with small gables, again as at Hymers College. In 1895 Boulevard School (290) was erected in this style, and shortly afterwards Northumberland Street Schools.

In 1902 the last of Bilson's Board Schools was erected. This was Wheeler Street School (296), which incorporates many features characteristic of his schools. The rather ugly tower has Jacobean-style slatted windows in its belfry stage, and the building as a whole cannot be compared with his earlier designs.

A study of the belfries which surmount many of Bilson's Board Schools is well worthwhile for these in many cases form the most beautiful feature of the buildings. The belfries of Buckingham Street (298), now demolished, and Westbourne Street Schools first show the design which he later perfected. Here the bases of the belfries are covered with slates; he later used lead to give a much neater appearance. The general effect here is one of clumsiness when compared with his later designs. The belfry of Stepney Schools (299) shows further development and refinement, and forms one of his most beautiful designs, later used as a clock tower at Hymers College. At Clifton Street Infants' School in 1888 he used a square belfry (300), now removed, which terminated without a weather vane. The square cupola was here supported by eight small Tuscan columns. At Malton Street he further developed the square belfry (301), supporting the upper part with pilasters at each corner, surmounted by an arch and pediment. The cupola here is more beautiful in design and terminates with a weather vane. In the case of Chiltern Infants' (302) and Middleton Street Infants', Bilson used small,

BOARD SCHOOLS

286 – BUCKINGHAM STREET

287 – MALTON STREET

288 – MIDDLETON STREET

289 – SCARBOROUGH STREET

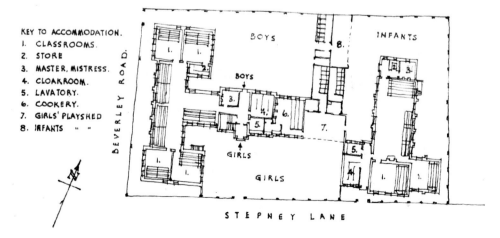

291 – STEPNEY

292 – CLIFTON STREET

290 – BOULEVARD

KEY TO ACCOMMODATION.
1. CLASSROOMS.
2. STORE
3. MASTER, MISTRESS.
4. CLOAKROOM.
5. LAVATORY.
6. COOKERY.
7. GIRLS' PLAYSHED
8. INFANTS " "

PLATE LII – STEPNEY BOARD SCHOOLS, 1886. ARCHITECT: JOHN BILSON

293 – Hull and Sculcoates
Dispensary,
Baker Street

294 – Chiltern Street Board
School

295 – Chiltern Street Board
School

296 – Wheeler
Street Board
School

297 – Hay's
Flour Mill,
Grosvenor
Street

Board School Belfries

298 – Buckingham
Street

299 – Stepney

300 – Clifton
Street Infants

301 – Malton
Street

302 – Chiltern
Street Infants

303 – Chiltern
Street

304 – Middleton
Street

305 – Scarborough
Street

306 – Scarborough
Street Infants

307 – Daltry
Street

308 –
HOUSE –
SALISBURY
STREET

309 –
HOUSE –
SALISBURY
STREET

310 –
HOUSES –
SALISBURY
STREET,
PARK
AVENUE

311 –
SHOPS –
PRINCES
AVENUE

312 –
CHARLOTTE
STREET

313 –
GROSVENOR
HOTEL,
CARR LANE

314 –
BRUNSWICK
CHAMBERS,
DOCK
STREET

315 –
HEPWORTH'S
ARCADE

316 –
OFFICES
– LAND
OF
GREEN
GINGER

317 –
OLYMPIC
CHAMBERS,
LAND OF
GREEN
GINGER

carefully designed octagonal belfries (302), based on his original belfry at Buckingham Street. For the main building at Chiltern Street he used a square two-tier belfry (303), the poorest of his designs. For the main building at Middleton Street he developed a pleasing octagonal belfry, whose cupola is surmounted by a small spire and weather vane (304). This was further developed for the senior school at Scarborough Street (305), although here the result was rather heavier. For Scarborough Street Infants' and Boulevard Schools, Bilson used a simple octagonal belfry with battered sides (306) and shouldered heads to the arches, rather clumsy and stumpy in appearance. The final development followed the pattern of Boulevard School, but with a spire instead of a cupola, rather cheap in appearance after some of the earlier examples. This was the design he used for extensions to Daltry Street (307), now demolished, and Williamson Street Schools. In the 1890s Bilson designed Hay's Flour Mill (297), in Grosvenor Street, now demolished, which showed how well he was able to adapt his basic style to an industrial building.

In 1884 George Gilbert Scott junior designed the group of fine Dutch-style houses in Salisbury Street, which links Westbourne and Park Avenues. Eight houses are arranged in a symmetrical layout, four in Salisbury Street proper, with another at each corner and one each in Westbourne and Park Avenues. The houses are constructed of red brick, with large stuccoed panels, and have attractive tiled roofs. They are all very large and of three storeys in height.

The middle block in Salisbury Street (308) comprises a pair of semi-detached houses. There is a projecting wing at each end of the symmetrical block, with a bay window on the ground floor, and the windows above terminating in a fine Dutch gable. The windows have wide box frames and are essentially Georgian in character. The first floor terminates with a heavy cornice, which surmounts a very fine decorative frieze carried out in stucco. The second-floor windows are all in the form of dormers. The entrance gateposts to these two houses are interesting, being quite monumental and Dutch in character, although the fine iron railings and gates which once graced these houses have now been removed. To either side of the semi-detached block is a fine double-fronted house (309) with bay windows to the ground floor and two fine Dutch gables to the second-floor windows. These houses are linked by an ornamental wall at ground-floor level to the corner house in each Avenue facing the fountains. The corner houses do not have Dutch gables (310); instead, the entrances are surmounted by towers rising to four storeys and terminated with cupolas. The towers are each flanked by two dormer windows, one on each side.

In both Westbourne and Park Avenues, one further detached double-fronted house completes the scheme. Some of the bay windows have had to be rebuilt because the hand-made bricks have decayed at the foundations. This has usually been done in a simplified manner, although the scheme as a whole remains externally much as Scott originally designed it.

Soon after these houses were built, a fine terrace of shops was erected in Princes Avenue (311). Although the shops are of a straightforward design carried out in red brick, the simple Dutch-style gables form an attractive pattern.

A number of buildings of predominantly Dutch appearance were also erected in the centre of the town in the late 1880s and early 1890s. Two shops in Charlotte Street (312), now demolished, had interesting gables in the Dutch tradition.

The Grosvenor Hotel (313), erected in Carr Lane in 1891 and now demolished, with Telephone House partly built on its site, was an interesting building with a Flemish touch, although predominantly Victorian in character. The balconies to the principal first-floor windows were quite gay in appearance. The elevation was, however, overwhelmed with detail, giving an impression of heaviness. The principal facing material was red stock bricks; the building also had stone dressings, a granite plinth and red granite columns supporting the ground-floor windows. The building was designed by Alfred Gelder.

Brunswick Chambers (314), in Dock Street, is similar in appearance to, but much smaller than, the Grosvenor Hotel. The building is quite interesting, but again gives a general impression of being overloaded with detail.

Hepworth's Arcade (315), in Silver Street, designed by Llewellyn Kitchen in 1894, is another typical example of the period, a thoroughly Victorian interpretation of the Dutch Renaissance style. This building is faced in stone, and the bays are constructed of timber.

The offices in Land of Green Ginger (316) provide another interesting example in the Dutch tradition. The building is noteworthy since it is almost entirely carried out in red brickwork, and is an excellent example of the use of moulded bricks.

Finally, Olympic Chambers (317), which was erected about 1895 to the designs of Smith and Brodrick, is an interesting building carried out in white Wallingfen stock bricks and cut stone. Built for W. M. Lewendon and Son, in Land of Green Ginger, it is typical of the period and has a Flemish feel. The original architect was Dudley Harbron, at that time articled to F. S. Brodrick. His design was in the Venetian style of the Dock Offices, by this time out of date. After Harbron had been working on the scheme for about a fortnight, Brodrick came to inspect the drawing board. 'Where's the door?' he asked. There was no door! Brodrick proceeded to modify the elevation with the result illustrated here.

CHAPTER X
THE THIRD GOTHIC REVIVAL

The last new parish church in the Ecclesiologist group was St Thomas's in 1882. No new church was then built in Hull until 1893, when the old church of St John, Newland, was extended.

The original church, erected in 1833, in the Early English style, to the designs of William Hutchinson, had by this time become inadequate for the rapidly expanding parish. To the existing building, which comprised a simple parallelogram of five bays, an additional bay was added, at the west end of the nave, together with a new chancel of two bays, and a north aisle to the nave (318). The alterations and extensions were carried out between 1893 and 1902 to the designs of Smith and Brodrick. The style is very different from that of earlier Hull churches and is much in line with that developed by George Gilbert Scott junior and George Frederick Bodley, and later continued by Temple Moore.

The general treatment is essentially Perpendicular in character. The small lancet windows by William Hutchinson, on the south side of the church, were replaced by the present, large three-light windows. The lancets on the north side were replaced by an arcade of six bays (321), giving access to the new north aisle which is lit by smaller three-light windows. The columns of the arcade have no capitals and the same mouldings continue up to form the arches.

The Tudor-shaped chancel arch (320) is carefully detailed, and the spandrels are ornamented with carved geometrical patterns. The form of the chancel arch is echoed in the timber trusses, which spring from stone corbels between the chancel windows. The chancel terminates with a fine five-light window of late Perpendicular style (319). The stonework at the sides of this window and of the chancel arch is bonded to the plasterwork, a feature usually reserved for the outside treatment of stone windows in brick walls. This feature was later used by Temple Moore in his two Hull churches.

The nave roof (320) is constructed of carved timber longitudinal and transverse ribs with plaster infilling. The roof terminates at the edges with a well-designed timber cornice ornamented with medallions and motifs which are picked out in colour. The organ is placed in a bay on the north side of the chancel.

The original part of the church was constructed on brick arches running transversely across the building, owing to the very poor subsoil close to the river Hull. The extensions were, however, built on ordinary brick footings and have settled rather badly; this settlement was accentuated by the effect of blast during the Second World War. Whilst it was unusual to use white stock bricks for church building at this time, Smith and Brodrick used them

here to harmonise with the existing building. It has a light and airy atmosphere, so refreshing after the darkness of earlier churches.

In the early 1890s Temple Moore took over Scott's work on the new church of St Augustine, and redesigned it in his own style. The main body of the church (322) and the base of the tower at the western end (324) were erected between 1890 and 1896; however, lack of money made it impossible to complete the tower as planned (LIII). The building, demolished in 1976, was faced externally with hand-made bricks, with an ornamental band composed of two courses of tiles about every tenth course. The copings and window tracery were executed in natural stone.

The interior (326), which comprised a nave of five bays with a north aisle and a chancel of two bays, had plastered walls throughout. A striking feature was the way in which the nave and chancel were housed under one roof, with the complete absence of a chancel arch. This gave the interior an effect of increased length and spaciousness and was an arrangement sometimes used by G. F. Bodley, for example, at St Augustine's, Pendlebury. However, in such instances, Bodley usually provided a light timber screen, forming a division between the nave and chancel; Temple Moore did not even use a screen here. At St Augustine's, however, the only difference between the general treatment of the nave and of the chancel was the reduction of the chancel windows on the south side from four lights (323) to three (325).

On the north side, the open arcade (328) terminated at the beginning of the chancel, and a smaller arch was provided in the first bay to accommodate the organ. The columns of the arcade (332) were simply though effectively handled. They had only partial capitals, with the front and back portions continuing up to form the arches, as at St John's, Newland. Small stone corbels on the north side of the arcade, of very weak appearance (328), supported the ugly and rather badly designed roof trusses of the north aisle.

The most beautiful feature of the church was undoubtedly its fine window tracery in the Decorated style. The seven-light window at the east end (326) was a beautiful example of Decorated tracery, and the curvilinear window at the west end (324) was almost as fine. The four-light windows on the south side of the nave (323) also had beautiful tracery, and the three-light curvilinear windows on the south side of the chancel (325) were reminiscent of some of the nave aisle windows of Beverley Minster. Interesting bonded corner stones were used to decorate the corners of the reveals to the interiors of the windows. The reveals continued down to the

318 – St John's, Newland – Exterior View

319 – Nave Looking East

320 – St John's, Newland – Chancel Arch

321 – Detail of Nave Arcade

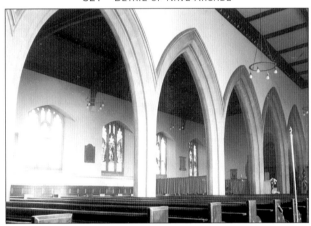

322 – St Augustine's – View from South-West

PLATE LIII – Church of St Augustine – Proposed West Tower. Architect: Temple Moore

324 – West Front

323 – Nave Window

325 – Chancel Window

326 – Nave looking East

327 – Detail of Roof

328 – North Aisle

329 – North Arcade

top of the oak-panelled dado, the walls below the windows being only half the thickness of the main walls. The simple boarded timber roof (327) rose from a substantial cornice on either side and was perhaps the most unhappy feature of the whole interior; rather harsh in its segmental treatment, it did not bear any real relationship to the beautiful curvature of the east and west windows.

The pulpit (330), with its sound-reflecting canopy above, was an interesting example of the timber work of this period. The carving on the pulpit, which was very pleasing, had no direct connection with any of the Gothic styles, and was an example of Temple Moore designing without constraint, guided only by his vigilant good taste. The oak panelling, choir stalls and altar rails were likewise designed in a style of Temple Moore's own invention.

Internally, the church was very pleasing, being light and airy, and the choice of external facing materials was excellent since the warm stonework contrasted beautifully with the mellowed hand-made bricks. Sadly the tower was never completed, although this would in turn have entailed the loss of the beautiful west window.

In 1912 St Nicholas' church (334), Hessle Road, was erected as a memorial to Edward VII, with money given by Christopher Pickering, a local benefactor. The church, which was very light and airy inside (336), was designed by John Bilson. However, this fine building was demolished in 1967 due to subsidence problems. The building comprised a tower at the west end, a nave of five bays with north and south aisles, and a chancel of two bays. The north and south aisles extended beyond one bay of the chancel, and the bay on the north of the chancel accommodated the organ.

It seems probable that Bilson was inspired by Temple Moore's earlier design for St Augustine's. Here, as at St Augustine's, the nave and chancel were both under one roof, with no intervening chancel arch or screen. The octagonal columns which supported the pointed arches of the arcade had no capitals. Their bases (333) and the mouldings of the arches, although on a much smaller scale, were the same as those used by Bilson at Hymers College some years earlier. The large arch at the west end, between the nave and tower, was supported by three-quarter piers at either side; the piers had similar bases and were the same size as those at Hymers College.

The general style of the church was Perpendicular, and the interior was plastered throughout. The east window of seven lights was of great beauty, although the tracery of this window and others throughout the building tended to be rather thicker and heavier than that of St Augustine's. However, the roof of the main body of the church (336) had been handled in a much better way. Springing from a stone cornice on either side, it was simply and effectively designed and finished in plaster. It took the form of a low arch which came to a point at the top and harmonised very well with the curvature of the arches of the east window and the western tower arch.

The aisles were roofed with almost flat timber ceilings, composed of transverse ribs with intermediate cross ribs, similar in character, but on a much smaller scale, to the aisle roofs of Holy Trinity. The aisle windows, with the exception of those to the north and south sides of the chancel aisles, had square heads and were of three lights (335). The windows of the aisles to the western bay of the nave were of two lights. Internally, the reveals of the windows continued to the floor, like those at St Augustine's, and the recesses thus formed accommodated the radiators.

The pews, which were simple in design, were beautifully executed in oak, and the pulpit (331) too was of great beauty. It was very similar to the pulpit at St Augustine's, made of oak, and with a fine sound-reflecting canopy. Both pulpits were octagonal in plan, although the carving to the pulpit at St Nicholas' was more Gothic in character.

The panelling to the chancel was of a simple, straightforward design and was well executed in oak. The altar reredos had a somewhat classical feel, although its simplicity harmonised very well with the design of the building as a whole. All the interior furniture, including the pulpit, was made in the workshops of Thompson of Kilburn, the celebrated Yorkshire wood-carver.

Externally, the church was forthright and bold. The facing materials used here were hand-made rustic bricks with stone dressings like those of St Augustine's; however, they were slightly more cherry red in colour, in contrast to St Augustine's brown-red. The simple treatment of the tower (334), with pilasters at each corner and battlemented termination, gave it a massive appearance and a very pleasing silhouette. The square-headed windows were very much in harmony with the whole design, and the reservation of pointed windows for places of prominence and emphasis was very subtle and very effective.

The slightly projecting bay of the south chancel aisle, with its pointed window and low pitched gable (335), admirably emphasised a change of use, and also formed an effective termination to the aisle. It almost gave the effect of being a transept. The aisles were effectively terminated at the western end against a small projecting buttress of the tower. The absence of buttresses did not give an effect of weakness; on the contrary, the simplicity of treatment, together with the horizontal parapet and square-headed windows, imparted a sense of unity and strength.

The tower was built on piles and the remainder of the church on brick footings. However, due to the poor subsoil, the body of the church sank rather badly; it was some six inches lower at the eastern than at the western end. Bad cracks showed

COMPARATIVE PULPITS

330 – PULPIT
ST AUGUSTINE'S

331 – PULPIT
ST NICHOLAS'S

COMPARATIVE PIERS

332 – PIER – ST AUGUSTINE'S

333 – PIER – ST NICHOLAS'

334 – ST NICHOLAS' – WEST FRONT

335 – ST NICHOLAS' – SOUTH AISLE

336 –
St Nicholas' –
Interior
looking
East

337 – St Mary's, Sculcoates – Nave looking East

338 – St Mary's, Sculcoates – Nave looking West

339 – St Mary's, Sculcoates – Nave Arcade

340 – St Mary's, Sculcoates – Chancel Arcade

considerable settlement of the west walls of the north and south aisles away from the tower, which had remained intact.

This was an excellent design of great beauty both inside and out, and a supreme example of a church in the Gothic style, planned with consideration for the contemporary requirements of clergy and congregation. It was undoubtedly finer than St Augustine's, and the presence of an arcade on both sides of the nave, lacking there, greatly enhanced the beauty of the interior. Bilson's understanding and knowledge of medieval architecture no doubt contributed largely to its success. This was the only church Bilson designed on his own account (although he had designed St Philip's, Hull, in conjunction with Botterill). Had he specialised in churches instead of schools, he would no doubt have become one of the leading ecclesiastical architects of the time. Nevertheless, St Nicholas' was undoubtedly the finest of all Hull churches of the Victorian period.

St Mary's, Old Sculcoates, designed by Temple Moore, was consecrated in 1916. It was built to replace the old church of St Mary, Sculcoates, which had become unsafe and was not worth repairing. The tower of the old church survived until the mid-1960s. Sheahan describes it in the following way, typical of its time: 'it is in the debased Gothic style of the tasteless period of its erection, and is entirely cased in compo.'

The foundation plate in the new church bears the following inscription:

To the Glory of God
and in place of the ancient Church of S. Mary,
which was taken down in the year 1915
This Church with its Chapels
of S. Francis and S. Patrick was Consecrated
By the Most Reverend
Cosmo Gordon, Lord Archbishop of York,
Primate and Metropolitan,
June 20th 1916.

Then follow the names of the vicar and churchwardens, and of Temple Moore, the architect. Like his earlier Hull church, St Augustine's, St Mary's has never been completed.

The exterior of the building is a simple structure faced in hand-made bricks with low pitched roofs and stone-mullioned windows, usually with square heads. The projected tower has never been started. The building comprises a nave of four bays (337) and a chancel of three bays (340), together with north and south aisles which continue along two bays of the chancel. The western bay of the south aisle was never completed and the corresponding bay of the north aisle was to have formed the base of the tower. To the north of the north aisle is the chapel of St Patrick (339), which comprises four bays smaller than those of the nave.

Many of the furnishings and fittings from the old church have been incorporated in the interior of the new. The circular columns which originally supported the nave arcades have been re-used here to form an inner arcade to St Patrick's chapel. The arches of the nave arcades are very wide; they are formed in plaster and rest on simple, oblong stone piers. The chancel arch is formed in plaster and has bonded stone quoins to the reveals. The crucifix is supported on a timber beam with ornamental brackets, and is reminiscent of the treatment used by George Gilbert Scott junior at St Agnes's, Kennington. The two arches on the south side of the chancel are supported by a simple stone pier, square in plan, with a stone capital which supports the pleasing arches moulded in plaster (340). The windows are all square headed and have either two or three lights, with the exception of the west windows of the nave and chapel of St Patrick. These are pointed and in the Decorated style, similar to, but smaller than, the south nave windows of St Augustine's (338). The arcades on the north side of the chancel, and between the north aisle and St Patrick's chapel, have simple semi-circular arches resting on square or octagonal stone piers.

The roof construction over the nave and chancel is rather weak and disappointing. The principal trusses spring from very weak and insignificant stone corbels, and longitudinal trusses span between the principals supporting the centre portion of the roof. The boarded roof, segmental in shape, springs from very weak timber cornices at each side. The nave and chancel have clerestory windows, a feature absent from the other three churches studied in this chapter. Two windows, each of two lights, surmount each bay of the nave and chancel. Two mural memorials in shorthand were among the most interesting monuments in the old church and were moved to the new building (339). The general aspect of the church is pleasing, although architecturally it does not compare well with St Augustine's. The simplicity of the design is effective, but as at St Augustine's, the roof is its most unsuccessful and disappointing feature.

341 – MUNICIPAL HOSPITALS, FOUNTAIN ROAD – GENERAL VIEW

343 – COURTYARD AND CHAPEL

342 – ENTRANCE GATEWAY

344 – ROYAL INSURANCE BUILDINGS, LOWGATE

345 – ROYAL INSURANCE BUILDINGS – ENTRANCE

346 – NATIONAL PROVINCIAL BANK, LOWGATE

347 – YORKSHIRE INSURANCE BUILDINGS, LOWGATE

CHAPTER XI

THE FINAL PHASE

The period between the middle of the 1880s and the First World War saw many trends, developments and architectural styles, and the buildings of this period are difficult to classify into well-defined architectural groups. It marked the peak of prosperity as well as of commercial and industrial expansion in the Victorian era, and the buildings erected at this time show a confusion of architectural whims, fancies and influences.

The turn of the century was a vital period in the architectural development of the centre of Hull. Queen Victoria Square was laid out as the new centre of the city, together with many adjoining new streets. In the last years or so of the 19th century the Old Town area had been substantially rebuilt, with offices and banks replacing the houses of earlier times. With all these factors in mind, the buildings of this complex period are discussed here in four sections, which together cover examples of all the important architectural trends then evident in Hull.

The Influence of Lowther

The partnership of Smith, Brodrick and Lowther (later Brodrick, Lowther and Walker) designed many of the buildings erected in the Old Town and elsewhere in Hull in the late 19th and early 20th centuries, and a large number of these designs are attributable to Arthur Lowther. Lowther rarely designed two buildings in the same style, and the origins of the styles he used are often difficult to trace, but all his buildings are very interesting and carefully detailed.

Lowther had worked for the firm since the 1870s and the earliest design which clearly displays his influence is the Municipal Hospitals (341), erected in Fountain Road, 1884-6. The siting of the almshouses near to the river Hull was bad and they were quickly surrounded by industries and factories of all kinds. However, the scheme, which comprises a continuous series of buildings on four sides of a courtyard (343), with an entrance gateway, is very fine. The building might best be described as Tudor in style.

The front elevation is a curious medley of timbered gables, and at each end is an unusual little octagonal tower surmounted by a short spire. The entrance gateway to the courtyard (342) is in the Tudor style and is surmounted by a fine stone oriel window. The entrance is emphasised by a partly timbered gable surmounted by an asymmetrical clock tower, indeterminate in style. This gateway is roofed with a very shallow brick arch, one of the most interesting features of the whole design. The small chapel in the late Gothic style (343), with its interesting belfry, is situated on the opposite side of the courtyard to the gateway. The buildings are constructed of brick with stone dressings, timber facings, tile hanging and tiled roofs. The scheme is carefully detailed throughout and forms a delightful haven of peace in what was at the time of writing an otherwise dreary and uninspiring industrial area of the city.

In 1890 York Union Bank (344), later the Royal Insurance Buildings, was designed by Lowther and erected at the corner of Bowlalley Lane and Lowgate. This building, since replaced with a new office block, was faced with Ancaster stone and roofed with ornamental tiles, and had a remarkably fresh appearance. The small octagonal cupola surmounting the corner entrance was very similar to the stages of the clock tower on Fountain Road almshouses. The two caryatids flanking the entrance (345) were particularly interesting, and the carved exterior stone friezes to each floor were worthy of study. Inside, the ceiling of the manager's office was a fine example of Victorian plasterwork, with the Greek egg-and-dart motif round the cornices.

The National Provincial Bank (346), at the corner of Lowgate and Scale Lane, and now a bar/restaurant, is another example of Lowther's work, and was erected in 1900. His use of the same materials and the expanses of plain ashlar stonework make it similar in general appearance to the Royal Insurance Building. However, on more careful study, the details are entirely different. This pleasing building is another example of Lowther's versatility in design.

About 1890 he designed Savile House (348), now partly demolished, at the corner of George Street and Savile Street, and Yorkshire Insurance Buildings in Lowgate (347), also now demolished. Both were constructed of red brick with stone dressings, and showed French and Venetian influences. As a composition Savile House is the better of the two designs, and the moulded brick corbels supporting the upper floors are interesting. However, the detailing of the windows of the Yorkshire Insurance Buildings (350) was better than at Savile House. Here dogtooth moulding and other ornament associated with English and French Gothic was profusely used, giving the windows a very rich appearance.

At about this time Lowther designed Cogan Chambers in Bowlalley Lane, home of Smith and Brodrick's offices for a number of years. The entrance (351) is the most striking feature of the whole design, and is interesting for its double treatment. The left-hand opening gives access to the offices and the right-hand opening gives access to Exchange Alley.

In 1891 Smith and Brodrick designed St Mary's Roman Catholic church, in Wilton Street, demolished in 1982, which had a double entrance doorway similar to the entrance to Cogan Chambers, but surmounted by a gable. St Gregory's Roman

348 – Savile House, Savile Street

349 – St Gregory's R.C. School, Scott Street

350 – Yorkshire Insurance Buildings – Window Details

351 – Cogan Chambers. Bowlalley Lane – Entrance

352 – Punch Hotel, Carr Lane

353 – Hull and Sculcoates Dispensary, Boulevard

Catholic school (349), erected in Scott Street in 1893, is very similar in character. The circular motif in the end gable containing flamboyant Gothic tracery could well be another example of Lowther's work.

In 1895-6 Smith, Brodrick and Lowther designed the Punch Hotel (352), in Carr Lane. This is perhaps the most flamboyant and exciting example of Lowther's work, constructed of hard red bricks with terracotta details. The bays are largely in the Elizabethan style, though the second-floor windows have more of a Gothic flavour and the gables are Flemish in character.

The western branch of Hull and Sculcoates Dispensary, in the Boulevard (353), was erected about the same time as the Punch Hotel and is faced in the same materials. It is a pleasing little building with a fine colonnade of three bays on the ground-floor, now bricked up. The whole design is very restrained when compared with the Punch Hotel.

The Influence of Norman Shaw

Norman Shaw, a leading architect of the 19th century, was an influential proponent of the Queen Anne Style.

The Police Station (355), erected 1902-4 in Alfred Gelder Street, was designed by J. H. Hirst, the City Architect at that time. It has now been largely demolished, although some fragments have been incorporated in the Littlewood's store which replaced it. It had a heavy hammered granite plinth, and the remainder of the building was faced with red brick and rusticated stonework. It is interesting to compare this building with the New Quadrant in Regent Street, London, built in the early 1920s to the designs of Sir Reginald Blomfield. A disciple of Shaw, Blomfield followed, with some modification, the style laid down by his master's earlier work in Regent Street. The general feeling of both elevations is the same and both have similar detailing. The New Quadrant in Regent Street is four storeys high and looks very fine, quite able to stand the heavy rusticated ground floor and rusticated first floor. Blomfield's double rusticated columns continued through three floors and the windows set back behind them had simple stone surrounds.

The Police Station in Hull was only two storeys high and was much over-weighted with heavy detail. Its double columns were rather stunted, continuing only through one floor, and for their size and height their rustications were too deep and their projections too pronounced. In addition, the first-floor windows between the columns had heavy rusticated stone architraves, making the building altogether too pompous. This was a typical example of the work of one of Norman Shaw's imitators, and showed what happened when his style was carried too far. It gave an appearance of strength suited to its purpose, but it was too pompous to be altogether pleasing.

The window treatment with a semi-circular glazing bar in the upper portion, used extensively by Norman Shaw, can be seen in many of the commercial buildings erected in Hull about 1900. Such treatment was often reserved for windows of particular prominence. The White Hart Hotel (369), in Alfred Gelder Street, was designed by Freeman, Son and Gaskell and shows a slightly later development in the terracotta style of public house design, typified by the Punch Hotel (352). Oriel Chambers, High Street (368), has a fine oriel window similar to that of the White Hart Hotel.

The former School Board Offices (354) erected 1896-8, at the junction of Albion Street and Union Street, is an imposing building in the Streaky Bacon style. It was designed by John Bilson and has a feeling of Norman Shaw, particularly on the Albion Street elevation. Here Bilson used rusticated columns and a central arch to his essentially Palladian window to the first floor. The entrance in Union Street (361) also has rusticated columns. The general treatment of this building is much more restrained in its detailing than was the Police Station and as a result the design is more dignified. This is the only building designed by Bilson which shows the direct influence of Norman Shaw.

In 1904 Edwin Rickards designed the Regional College of Art on Anlaby Road (356). Two years earlier Rickards designed Deptford Town Hall, and the elevational treatment of both these buildings is very similar. The College of Art has three principal floors and the ground floor is raised on a semi-basement. The entrance (358) is approached by a flight of steps, flanked by a wing wall terminating with a square stone pedestal surmounted by a fine iron lamp. The entrance portico, which is surmounted by the windows and the balcony to the principal's study, is entirely executed in Ancaster stone, being oval in plan and supported by two columns of the Tuscan order. The windows have attractively designed stone architraves, and the centre block terminates with a pediment containing a picture portraying the arts in coloured mosaics, designed by Garth Jones, and executed by Bromsgrove Arts Guild. It is protected by a large overhanging roof.

Inside, the studios and other rooms are grouped around the fine central staircase hall (357), with galleries giving access to the upper floors. The main hall is on the ground floor opposite the main entrance. It is slightly below the level of the entrance hall, and a short flight of steps leads down to its entrance. These are flanked by two Tuscan columns and surmounted by a semi-circular opening containing a wrought iron balustrade bearing the date 1904. Behind the balustrade is the staircase leading to the upper floors. The first-floor balcony is ornamented with Tuscan columns which support a cornice above. The floors of the entrance

354 – SCHOOL BOARD OFFICES, ALBION STREET

355 – POLICE STATION, ALFRED GELDER STREET

356 – REGIONAL COLLEGE OF ART, ANLABY ROAD

357 – REGIONAL COLLEGE OF ART – ENTRANCE HALL

358 –
REGIONAL
COLLEGE
OF ART,
ENTRANCE

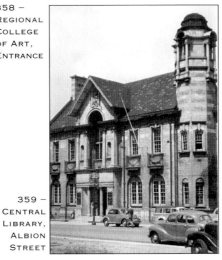

359 –
CENTRAL
LIBRARY,
ALBION
STREET

360 –
CENTRAL
LIBRARY –
ENTRANCE

361 –
SCHOOL
BOARD
OFFICES

362 –
MARKET
HALL,
NORTH
CHURCH
SIDE

363 –
PUBLIC
BATHS,
BEVERLEY
ROAD

PLATE LIV – New Market Hall and Corn Exchange, 1902. architect: J. W. hirst, city architect's department

364 – Town Hall Chambers, Alfred Gelder Street

365 – Maritime Buildings, Alfred Gelder Street

366 – Market Hall, North Church Side

367 – Northern Library, Beverley Road

368 – ORIEL CHAMBERS, HIGH STREET

369 – WHITE HART HOTEL, ALFRED GELDER STREET

370 – EMPRESS HOTEL, ALFRED GELDER STREET

371 – SHOPS – JAMESON STREET

PLATE LV – STRAND PICTURE THEATRE, BEVERLEY ROAD. ARCHITECTS: MESSRS WELLSTED AND DOSSOR

hall and the landings are finished in terrazzo. The design of the building throughout is of a very high standard, and the admirable proportions and careful treatment of the front elevation distinguish it as one of Hull's finest buildings of the later Victorian era.

The Central Library (359), erected in Albion Street in 1900, and extended 1959-62, was designed by J. S. Gibson, of London, and has a prominent central entrance (360), executed entirely in stone. Whilst similar in style to the Regional College of Art, this building is much inferior in design. The central entrance is very top-heavy and the portico appears squashed by the great weight above it. The proportion of the first floor to the ground floor is very poor. The heavy cornice over the entrance is almost two-thirds its height. The Ionic columns to the portico are badly proportioned and have insufficient entasis. The window above is deeply recessed, thus giving it an extra heavy appearance. The pilasters flanking this window are large and out of scale when compared with the columns flanking the entrance below.

The treatment of the windows on either side of the entrance, however, is very pleasing. The octagonal tower added to the otherwise symmetrical elevation has the appearance of being stuck on. Instead of making the design asymmetrical, the tower gives it a one-sided effect. It may well have been inspired by the tower of the Indian Institute at Oxford, designed by Basil Champneys in 1882.

The new Market Hall and Corn Exchange (LIV), on the north side of Holy Trinity, was erected 1902-4, to the designs of J. H. Hirst. Constructed of red hand-made bricks and Ancaster stone, the principal elevation of this building is of outstanding merit (362). The tower at the east end of the elevation is its most beautiful feature and accommodates the staircase leading to the Corn Exchange Hall at first-floor level. The lower portion of the tower is very simple, mainly of brick, and is surmounted by a fine stone campanile terminating with a dome. The general treatment of the tower is similar to that of the Public Library, but here the simplicity and good proportion of the design are far superior.

Beverley Road Baths (363), built in 1905, and similarly designed by Hirst, also have a domed campanile surmounting the main entrance, but here the effect is rather one of clumsiness and bad proportion when compared with the Market Hall.

The main façade of the Market Hall (366) has fine semi-circular headed entrances at ground-floor level, separated by wide, slightly projecting piers which continue as pilasters through the elevation of the upper floor. The windows of the upper floor are of three lights and have stone mullions and transoms, together with small bow-shaped balconies which each have a simple, delicate wrought iron railing. The piers between the ground-floor entrances and the pilasters are ornamented with carved stone medallions. The whole design is of a very high standard, and is in pleasing and carefully selected materials. This building, together with Beverley Road Baths and the Central Library, has a very Continental flavour typical of many of the buildings erected about this time and befitting Hull's position as one of the country's leading ports.

In 1902 Town Hall Chambers (364) was erected at the corner of Alfred Gelder Street and Quay Street. This very fine building is a good example of the work of Llewellyn Kitchen. Constructed of red brick with Ancaster stone dressings, it is very refined in its detailing and today has much of the mellowed charm and appearance of a Georgian building.

Maritime Buildings (365), 1904, also in Alfred Gelder Street, was designed by W. S. Walker of Brodrick, Lowther and Walker, and is no less beautiful. The curved façade of the building, in the same materials as Town Hall Chambers, is particularly fine. An interesting feature of the design is the way in which the chimneys are emphasised as pilasters used to punctuate the elevation. Originally the pairs of chimney stacks at each end had intervening gables containing circular windows. The interior of the building was gutted by fire bombs during the Second World War, and the chimney stacks and part of the parapet have since been rebuilt. The chimney stacks originally terminated in a manner similar to those of Town Hall Chambers.

The Empress Hotel (370) in Alfred Gelder Street by J. H. Hirst, was erected in 1903; its ground floor has now been altered. About the same time a beautiful group of three shops (371), now demolished, was also erected in Jameson Street. The general appearance of both these buildings is very similar. Beautiful chimney stacks, with tall slender pots, emphasise the height of both designs. Both buildings were constructed of brick and had interesting decorative horizontal bands in stucco, bearing delicate and attractive detailing. The ground floor of the Empress Hotel was similar in style to its contemporary, the White Hart Hotel (369), in Alfred Gelder Street, erected in 1904.

The Jameson Street shops were the more beautiful of the two buildings. The mansard roofs between the gables of the upper floor were faced with green Westmorland slates. The rainwater heads were also of a very interesting design.

Northern Library on Beverley Road (367), by Cheers of Twickenham, is another interesting building, erected in 1895. It is difficult to identify it with any one style; however, it is remarkable for its wealth of turrets, spires and other details, which at the same time do not give its comparatively small elevation an overcrowded appearance.

Lee's Rest Houses, on Anlaby High Road (374), are a fine Neo-Georgian ensemble. A trust was formed after Dr Charles A. Lee, who died in 1912, left almost all his fortune, amounting to £95,000, to build and endow some rest homes. A competition

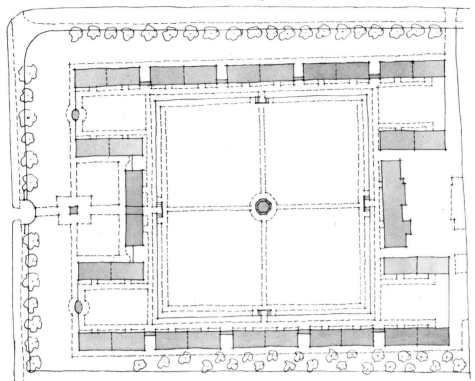

PLATE LVI – Lee's Rest Houses, Anlaby Road, 1915. architect: H. T. Hare

372 – Lee's Rest Houses – Entrance

373 – Centre Shelter

374 – General View

375 – Garden Shelter

was held, and the design of Henry T. Hare, a London architect, was accepted. The illustration (LVI) shows the general arrangement of the scheme, which was officially opened on 10th September 1915. The blocks surround a large quadrangle. Each block contains accommodation for eight residents. On the south side of the quadrangle is a central block containing a fine room, 50 feet by 25 feet, panelled in oak, which is used as a chapel and reading room. This block also houses the board room, a room for the medical officer, and a replica of Dr Lee's dining room, at his private residence in Pryme Street, Hull. There are altogether 30 blocks, each containing four flats. Each flat contains a living room with a bay window; a bedroom; a scullery, with hot and cold water; a coal house; and a pantry. In addition, there are two WCs and one bathroom to each block. The blocks, which are in pairs, are linked by covered shelters (375), and the shelter in the centre of the quadrangle contains a dovecot (373). The entrance archway (372) is the most beautiful feature of the whole scheme, forming the central feature of the front block. The buildings, which are in beautiful surroundings, formed one of the finest such schemes in the country for their period, and were considered by the Charity Commission as a model design.

The Strand Picture Theatre (LV), on Beverley Road, designed by Wellsted and Dossor, was destroyed by fire and had been demolished by the mid-1960s. It was a good example of cinema design of the period, quite refined in its treatment and displaying some influence of the Queen Anne style.

From 1907 onwards Garden Village was developed. The scheme, designed by Percy T. Runton and William E. Barry, was sponsored by Sir James Reckitt, as a conveniently situated estate in pleasing surroundings for those who worked for Reckitt and Colman. The site which was chosen was only about half a mile from the factory and is located in the former grounds of Holderness House. A fine avenue of well-matured elm trees, which originally led to the main entrance of Holderness House, forms the principal avenue of the estate, and is known as Elm Avenue. To the east of Elm Avenue, the Oval opens out. This forms the centre of the scheme and is rather like a large village green (380), surrounded as it is by a number of houses. The houses are all in the style of Charles Voysey, the leading architect of the 'Garden Village' movement, and are very pleasing; all kinds of designs are well mixed together (381, 382). The avenues are all named after trees; for example, Lilac Avenue, Lime Tree Avenue and Laburnum Avenue.

A charming feature of the scheme is the Shopping Centre (376), which was erected in 1909. In the Georgian style, it is 'E' shaped in plan, and constructed of red brick with extensively rendered façades. The main entrance (376, 378) is through a large archway, surmounted by a small clock tower, which gives access to a courtyard, surrounded on three sides by a fine colonnade, supported by columns of the Tuscan order (377, 379). Under the colonnade are the shops. The fourth side of the courtyard is open to Beech Avenue. The first-floor windows overlooking the courtyard have ornamental shutters. As a whole the Garden Village estate today forms one of the most pleasant residential areas within the city boundary.

Between 1900 and 1910, a number of three-storey houses were erected in various parts of Hull which show something of the influence of Norman Shaw. A number of these are to be found in Newland Park, which was being developed at this time. Others were built on Anlaby High Road and in the Avenues, in particular Westbourne Avenue and Victoria Avenue. The group of three houses in Westbourne Avenue (383), is the best example and is similar in many ways to Shaw's Hostelry in Bedford Park, London, the earliest of the garden villages.

A New Gothic Style

Towards 1890 a simplified Gothic style came into use for certain public buildings. It was later used for many of the Nonconformist churches erected at the beginning of the 20th century, sometimes tending towards Art Nouveau. Many of the buildings in this style were designed by Alfred Gelder. Earlier examples were usually in red brick and stone, or they were completely stone faced, but later terracotta and, in some cases, glazed yellow bricks were used.

The earliest building in this group is James Reckitt Public Library (LVII), Holderness Road, which was erected in 1889. It was designed by Alfred Gelder and is faced with red stock bricks and Ancaster and Howley Park stone dressings. It is in a simple and very pleasing Gothic style. The principal entrance is surmounted by a tower terminating in an octagonal steeple with a weather vane and an octagonal geometrical pinnacle at each corner. On the first floor is a fine oriel window carried out in stone. Taken as a whole, the building is very pleasing, although the tower lost its pinnacles and spire during the Second World War and they have not been replaced. Another of Gelder's buildings in this style is Paragon Arcade (384), which connects Paragon Street and Carr Lane, and was built in 1892. Constructed of similar materials, its eaves were originally ornamented with four stone pinnacles, similar to those of James Reckitt Library, but they became unsafe and were removed in the early 1950s. The entrance to the arcade continues through two storeys of the building, and each of the shops has a Gothic window on the first floor. The delicate cast iron trusses (385) which span the arcade are the most beautiful feature of the whole design. The first-floor walls of the interior of the arcade are an interesting example of the Streaky Bacon style.

Between 1895 and 1910 a number of

376 – GARDEN VILLAGE – SHOPPING CENTRE

378 – GARDEN VILLAGE – MAIN ENTRANCE

379 – GARDEN VILLAGE – COLONNADE

377 – GARDEN VILLAGE – VIEW OF SHOPS

380 – GARDEN VILLAGE – THE OVAL

381 – GARDEN VILLAGE – HOUSES

382 – Houses – Garden Village

383 – Houses – Westbourne Avenue

384 – Paragon
Arcade, Carr
Lane

384 – Paragon
Arcade – Detail
of Roof

386 – St
James's Parish
Institute

387 – Argyle
Street Wesleyan
Chapel

Nonconformist churches were erected in Hull. The earliest of these was Argyle Street Wesleyan (387), 1895, now demolished, which was designed by Alfred Gelder. It was constructed of red stock bricks and was the first church in Hull where terracotta dressings were used instead of natural stone. The horizontal terracotta bands showed something of the influence of William Butterfield. The general approach to the design was Early Christian in feel. Essentially the plan requirements were the same as those of earlier Methodist churches; here the staircases leading to the upper galleries were placed in small wings at the sides of the main block.

In 1899 Fish Street Memorial Congregational church (388), Prince's Avenue, now the Elim Pentecostal City Temple, was erected to the designs of W. H. Bingley. It is constructed of red stock bricks with cut stone dressings, similar in style to James Reckitt Library and Paragon Arcade. However, the front elevation is marred by a confusion of units of varying shapes and sizes. Although the windows and entrances are carefully detailed, the central lancet below the rose window serves only to spoil the elevation. The octagonal tower gives a one-sided effect to the design and is balanced on the other side by a weak pinnacled buttress which has the effect of being stuck on. The whole design is rather piecemeal and lacks unity.

In 1907 Bingley designed Boulevard United Methodist church, which was constructed of red stock bricks and terracotta dressings. Inferior in design to Fish Street church, it is again rather piecemeal and lacking in unity. The church was demolished in the late 1980s.

In 1903 a competition was held for the design of the proposed new Baptist church to be erected at the corner of Trafalgar Street and Beverley Road. Alfred Gelder entered the competition but was unsuccessful, and the church was built to the designs of George Baines and Son, London, 1904-6 (389). This is the only building in Hull which shows Art Nouveau influence to any real degree. It is faced with flint and the details are picked out in very red bricks. The roofs are covered in tile and the curious spire is covered with lead. The design as a whole is an exciting example of Art Nouveau Gothic. Doubtless the promoters were very pleased with it for they erected another church in Liverpool to the same designs.

Queen's Hall (390), demolished in 1965, was erected in 1905, in Alfred Gelder Street, to the designs of Alfred Gelder. This building also had something of an Art Nouveau Gothic feel to its front elevation, entirely executed in stone. The ground floor comprised six shops, three on either side of the main entrance to the hall. The elevation was effectively terminated at each end with a cupola which surmounted the subsidiary entrances to the building. The elevation as a whole was very pleasing, and the tower surmounting the entrance was well handled. In massing it was very similar to the Liver Building in Liverpool. The upper windows, with their Gothic style tracery, lit the offices which were rather awkwardly placed behind them. The entrance foyers and staircases were very disappointing after the rather fine exterior; they were entirely faced with glazed bricks, giving more the appearance of a London subway than the entrance to the headquarters of Hull Methodist Mission. The hall itself was better than the entrances, but this was a good example of a building where most of the money had been spent on the façade.

In 1905 Alfred Gelder was commissioned to design Princes Avenue Wesleyan church. It is instructive to compare the designs for this building (391) with Gelder's unsuccessful entry for Trafalgar Street Baptist church two years earlier: the elevations are almost identical. The front elevation of Trafalgar Street church was flanked by two towers terminating with spires; however, owing to the triangular nature of the Princes Avenue site, one of the towers was omitted in the new design. It is interesting to note here how Gelder made use of his competition design, chopping it down slightly and adding bits on here and there to fit the new site.

The design of the tower and spire is very pleasing, and the four corner turrets are very similar to the cupolas of Queen's Hall. The tracery of the principal window is also similar to the windows of Queen's Hall, although slightly more comprehensive. However, the entrance porch is rather large and tends to reduce the apparent scale of the rest of the building. The hard red bricks together with the cleanly weathered stone gives the building a comparatively new appearance. Part of this building survives, incorporated into a new church building on the site.

In 1910 Gelder designed Plane Street Wesleyan chapel, Anlaby Road, in the same materials. The general style of the window tracery is Decorated Gothic, although in massing and composition the design is less successful than Princes Avenue church. This building, which was in a derelict state, was demolished in 2004 and the site has been redeveloped.

In 1903 Boulevard Baptist church (393), demolished in the 1970s, was erected in Gordon Street. It was designed by Brownlow Thompson and was an interesting example of his later work. It was a fine example of massing and composition, and the octagonal tower and spire were well designed. The choice of materials, glazed yellow bricks with red brick dressings, was unusual and gave the building a cold and unfriendly appearance.

In 1904-6 Newland Congregational church (394) was erected on Beverley Road, at the corner of Vermont Street. It was designed by Moulds and Porritt, of Bury, Manchester and London, and was demolished – the east end apart – in 1969. Constructed of hard red and yellow bricks with

PLATE LVII – JAMES RECKITT LIBRARY,
HOLDERNESS ROAD, 1889.
ARCHITECT: W. ALFRED GELDER.

388 – FISH STREET MEMORIAL
CONGREGATIONAL CHURCH

389 – TRAFALGAR STREET BAPTIST CHURCH

390 – QUEEN'S HALL, ALFRED GELDER STREET

392 – GERMAN LUTHERAN CHURCH, NILE STREET

391 – PRINCES AVENUE WESLEYAN CHURCH

393 –
BOULEVARD
BAPTIST
CHURCH

394 – NEWLAND CONGREGATIONAL CHURCH – GENERAL VIEW

395 – FRONT ELEVATION   396 – INTERIOR

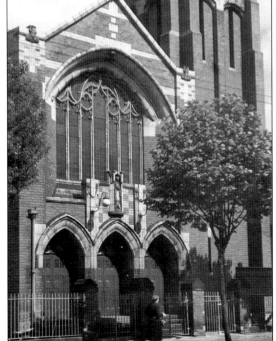

397 – City Hall – East Front

398 – City Hall – Detail of Side Elevation

399 – City Hall – Art Gallery

400 – City Hall – South Elevation

401 – Seaton Building, Paragon Square

402 – Shop – Prospect Street

403 – Shop – Prospect Street

404 – Gelder and Kitchen's Offices, Alfred Gelder Street

405 – Post Office, Alfred Gelder Street

406 – French Convent School, Park Grove

407 – French Convent School, Main Entrance

408 – Shops – Prospect Street

409 – Yorkshire Penny Bank, Queen Victoria Square

terracotta dressings to the windows, it was a strong, simple and graceful composition and was an interesting example of massing. It was remarkable for the innovatory series of figures of 19th-century Free Church leaders on the outside of the tower. These included a statue of Dr Livingstone, but their placing was unfortunate, tending to break the graceful vertical lines of the tower, which rose to 120 feet. The church was octagonal in plan. The window tracery (395) was interesting and showed the influence of the Art Nouveau movement. The interior (396) was rather disappointing after the exterior and had a somewhat cold and unfriendly feel.

The German Lutheran church in Nile Street (392) was rebuilt in 1911, to the design of Oswald Hillerns, a chartered engineer and partner in the family firm of seed and corn merchants. Now demolished, it was an interesting small building, with a distinctly German Renaissance feeling about its little tower and cupola. The simple geometrical tracery to the west window was interesting and very effective. The general treatment of the entrance, the west window and the gable, was that used by Alfred Gelder for Argyle Street Wesleyan 15 years earlier. This was an unpretentious building but nonetheless interesting for its effective use of simple mouldings and details.

Edwardian Exuberance

The reign of King Edward VII saw something of a rebirth of the English Renaissance style for new civic and commercial buildings.

The first building in this style was City Hall (397), designed by J. H. Hirst, and erected in Queen Victoria Square, 1903-9. This building is an interesting example of the results of a hybrid programme – something that should never happen in architectural practice. The original requirements of the programme were for a large hall, together with foyers and other ancilliary accommodation. A design for a building on these lines was drawn up; however, it was then decided that, since this area was developing as the new shopping centre, it might be appropriate to provide shops under the new hall. The design was raised up and shops were so placed, considerably reducing the civic dignity of the building. The entrance was then amended to suit these new requirements and a heavy stone portico added. It was later decided to incorporate an art gallery in the design; a further section, also placed above shops, was therefore added at the rear (399, 400), and a connecting doorway provided. However, the only access to the art gallery was now via the hall, which would be very unsatisfactory. An awkward, tight entrance staircase was therefore worked into the Carr Lane elevation to give access to the gallery. This entrance, which can be seen on the left of the illustration (398), bears no relation to the remainder of the elevation. The art gallery is

lighted by roof lights only, and the walls outside are divided into panels bearing carved stone portraits and the names of prominent artists through the ages (399).

The most pleasing feature of the exterior of this hybrid design is the fine dome (397) which surmounts the entrance portico. The finest feature of the interior is the entrance staircase, executed in coloured marbles. It is very similar in arrangement to, and was doubtless inspired by, the main staircase in Brodrick's Town Hall.

The French Convent School (406), in Park Grove, off Princes Avenue, now demolished, was erected shortly after City Hall. It was an attractive building, constructed of white stock bricks and stone dressings, with nicely detailed window heads. The segmental stone window heads were similar to those used on City Hall, although much more delicate. The entrance (407) was in the Renaissance style and terminated with a segmental pediment.

Between 1903 and 1906 a number of buildings faced in Ancaster stone were designed in a semi-Renaissance style by Gelder and Kitchen. The Seaton Building, in Paragon Square (401), was one of the most outstanding examples of their work in this style, although today a small portion remains of the original scheme (401). The Prospect Street shop, with its green copper dome (402), is another interesting example of this style; another shop front (403), also in Prospect Street, shows its further development, which tends to be rather top-heavy.

Gelder and Kitchen's own offices, in Alfred Gelder Street (404), now demolished, were probably the most interesting development of this style. Although exciting, the design appeared unstable and top-heavy. The ground floor was given over to a series of shops, with an unusual narrow entrance leading to the offices on the upper floors. Books were later found in Gelder and Kitchen's offices showing similar contemporary German buildings and it seems probable that these influenced this design.

The new General Post Office (405), in Alfred Gelder Street, was erected 1908-9. It was designed by W. Potts of HM Office of Works and is a dull building constructed in Portland stone. The design is all very much the same with no dominating feature or focal point. The principal entrance is in the centre of the Lowgate elevation but its insignificance makes it difficult to find.

In 1904 work began on the new Law Courts in Alfred Gelder Street (410) following a competition won by Sir Edwin Cooper. From an architectural point of view, the site of the building was hopeless from the start. Very narrow, it is 560 feet long and included the site of Brodrick's Town Hall, together with land to the west. The whole of the new building, which includes the Law Courts and the Town Hall, is known as the Guildhall. The Law Courts, which occupy the whole of the site west of the old Town Hall, have their principal elevation

410 – Law Courts, Alfred Gelder Street

411 – Law Courts – Detail of Elevation

412 – Guildhall – Main Front

413 – Guildhall – Side Elevation

414 – Law Courts – End Termination

415 – Law Courts – Main Entrance

facing Alfred Gelder Street. This façade is symmetrical, with the principal entrance in the centre (415), and each end is terminated with a slightly projecting block, from which rises a group of sculptures (414) representing maritime progress and strength. Only a few of the greatest architects have been able satisfactorily to handle long façades and here the result is weak and uncoordinated. The building faces a comparatively narrow street; had it faced an open square or park the result might have been more satisfactory. The central entrance (415) is insufficiently important for its function on so extensive a façade, and would have been much improved had it been surmounted with a tower. It is a great pity that the assessor did not comment on the unsuitability of the site from an architectural point of view; no doubt a better site could have been chosen.

About 1912 Brodrick's beautiful Town Hall was pulled down to make way for a new Guildhall to harmonise with the Law Courts. This was a barbarous act; the Guildhall is inferior even to the design of the Law Courts, to which it is linked by a nondescript conglomeration of windows of varying sizes, and by pilasters of rusticated stonework (410). The principal entrance (412) – in the centre of the east elevation, as in Brodrick's design – is very coarse and undignified and is surmounted by a rather ugly clock tower. The lower part of the tower is in Ancaster stone, in harmony with the remainder of the building, while the upper stages are in Portland stone. The detailing of the building is coarse and clumsy throughout and cannot be compared with contemporary masterpieces such as Cardiff City Hall and Law Courts, 1897, by Edwin Rickards.

About 1910 there was a return to terracotta for the many shops and other commercial buildings being erected in the newly laid-out streets. The shops in Prospect Street (408) are a typical example, faced in glazed red bricks with white terracotta dressings. The treatment of the tall gables has something of a Flemish appearance. These shops were designed by Freeman, Son and Gaskell. The Yorkshire Penny Bank, now the Yorkshire Bank, by B. S. Jacobs, c.1900, in Queen Victoria Square (409), is another example of a commercial building, this time faced entirely in buff-brown terracotta above a red granite plinth.

CONCLUSION

To many people Kingston upon Hull appears a typical industrial city, with very little of interest or beauty. Many of the buildings studied here stand side by side with others which have no architectural qualities or merit. Many of the churches, chapels and schools, for instance, are situated in long, straight streets containing endless, monotonous terraces of red brick houses, which are examples only of building and not of architecture. But in spite of the general aspect of much of the town, Hull in 1955 still had an extremely rich heritage of fine buildings erected in the Victorian era.

Many of these buildings were designed by famous architects from London and elsewhere, but many more are the work of a strong backbone of talented local architects, who throughout the period were able to achieve remarkable feats with local materials. George Pycock set a high architectural standard in the 1790s, and this was later continued by Charles Mountain junior, a fine local architect.

Mountain was followed by H. F. Lockwood, who designed the greatest number of Hull's finest buildings of this period. Many of his best works have now been lost for ever, but it is to be hoped that those which still remain will be carefully preserved. It was Lockwood who trained the young Cuthbert Brodrick in the profession of architecture. There is no doubt that his years with Lockwood were extremely profitable to him, for shortly afterwards he became one of the leading architects of the Victorian era.

The work of Joseph Wright was generally of a high standard. Samuel Musgrave designed two chapels in the classical manner, but achieved outstanding success locally from the 1870s onwards by designing churches and other buildings after the manner of G. E. Street.

William Botterill also designed a large number of buildings of interest. However, it was his pupil John Bilson who was later to become famous as a designer of schools and colleges, and Hull retains many of his fine schools. Bilson was also the prime mover in the introduction of the Dutch and Flemish Renaissance styles to Hull. Alfred Gelder and his partner, Llewellyn Kitchen, were the last of Hull's fine series of local architects of the Victorian era and designed many interesting buildings in the latter part of this period.

Hull, as we have seen, was titled the 'Venice of England'. As an almost flat city, it depends essentially on its skyline for its interest and beauty, and it is not surprising that many buildings of this period were surmounted by domes, towers or steeples. Seen in 1955 from the middle of the River Humber the skyline of the city certainly resembled the skyline of Venice.

Hull is still passing through a period of transition and reconstruction even though the effects of the Second World War have long since passed. Many of the long, uninspiring streets with their overcrowded houses unfit for habitation have now been removed and replaced with new housing. The demolition of a large number of interesting buildings throughout the city has already taken place, but it is to be hoped that some of the outstanding examples still remaining will be preserved. It might be possible in some cases to develop new schemes using some of the finest buildings of the Victorian era as focal points, showing their qualities to an advantage impossible before. Some of these buildings are of outstanding merit and well worth preserving for future generations to see and enjoy. It is to be hoped that in such instances any which do become redundant can be adapted sensitively to new uses rather than being demolished. It is pleasing to report that, in the years since this work was first written, there are gratifying signs of progress.

BIBLIOGRAPHY

Early Marine Paintings and Hull Art Directory, Hull, Ferens Art Gallery, 1951.

Allison, Keith J. ed. *The Victoria History of the County of York, East Riding:* I *Kingston-upon-Hull*, University of London, 1969.

Bilson, John 'Kingston-Upon-Hull in 1293', *Transactions of the East Riding Antiquarian Society*, 26, 1929, 37-105.

Clarke, B. F. L. *Church Builders of the Nineteenth Century*, SPCK, 1938.

Cowen, H. M. *Biographical Dictionary of British Architects*, 1660-1840, Murray, 1978.

Gillett, E. and MacMahon K. A. *History of Hull*, University of Hull Press, 1980.

Hall, Ivan and Elisabeth *Georgian Hull*, York, Sessions, in conjunction with Hull Civic Society, 1978-9.

Harbron, G. D. FRIBA 'Notes on some Architects of the 18th Century', *Transactions of the Georgian Society for East Yorkshire*, 2 (4), 1948-9, 22-32.

Ketchell, C. ed. *An Illustrated History of the Avenues and Pearson Park*, The Avenues and Pearson Park Residents' Association, 1989.

Neave, D. *Lost Churches and Chapels of Hull*, Hull City Museums and Art Galleries and Hutton Press, 1991.

Pevsner, N. and Neave, D., *The Buildings of England: Yorkshire, York and the East Riding*, 2nd edition, Penguin, 1995.

Sheahan, J. J. *History of the Town and Port of Kingston-upon-Hull*, Beverley, John Green, 2nd ed., 1866.

Thompson, A. Hamilton, 'Obituary to John Bilson', *RIBA Journal*, 51, 1943-4, 94.

INDEX

INDEX OF NAMES

Note: references in **bold** are to the biographical sketches in Chapter
2; references in *italic* are to the page number of the illustrations.

INDEX OF BUILDINGS, STREETS, ETC.